Practical Eco-Electrical Home Power Electronics

D. Fichte

Practical
Eco-Electrical Home Power Electronics

D. Fichte

Elektor International Media BV
P.O. Box 11
6114 ZG Susteren
The Netherlands

British Library Cataloguing in Publication Data
A catalogue record for this book is available from the British Library

ISBN 978-0-905705-83-5

Prepress production: Kontinu, Sittard
Design cover: Helfrich Ontwerpbureau, Deventer
First published in the United Kingdom 2009
Printed in the Netherlands by Wilco, Amersfoort
© Elektor International Media BV 2009

099016-UK

Table of Contents

Off-Grid System Strategy

The companion book to this one, *Your own Eco-Electrical Home Power System*, combined existing commercial power-system components without redesigning or modifying the design of any of them. Hints were given that a more optimal system could be devised with some additional electronics skills. This book assumes that you have such skills and are willing to experiment with both component and system development.

12 V Systems

Residential off-grid systems are often based on a bank of 12 V batteries. The most commonly available and affordable deep-discharge batteries, such as those found in fork lifts or for golf carts, are either 6 V or 12 V. Although it is not difficult to place these batteries in series, many other system components are not designed to operate on higher voltages.

What is undesirable about 12 V systems is the high current needed for significant power. A 1500 W inverter will draw about 150 A from the battery bank. At this current, wire size is typically from 6 to 2 AWG and must be kept short. High currents also require very good connections, and with time and thermal cycling, connector resistances can increase, leading to power loss and possible connector failure. Connectors must be checked occasionally for tightness. And not the least concern is that large-diameter copper wires are also expensive.

The automotive industry has for years been talking about going to 36 V batteries (or a 42 V bus), or three 12 V batteries in series. For the same power, the current is reduced to a third. The choice of a 42 V battery bus voltage is based in part on safety; 42 V is under what the safety standard considers a safe voltage. A few decades ago, the 'safe threshold' voltage was considered to be around 42 V. It has since been increased to around 50 V. Thus, a 48 V battery system might still be safe, though in practice, transient voltages approaching this safety threshold occur in 42 V automotive systems using 36 V batteries. Consequently, the 42 V lead-acid battery bus is the practical upper limit that avoids unsafe 'high voltage'.

In a user-designed home electric system, you decide what is safe, especially if you live where government does not (or could not) micromanage such decisions. The choice of a 42 V battery bus for safety, however, concurs with established safety organizations and is consequently a recommended guideline for home system design. The alternative system, shown in the next section, uses a 36 V battery bank as a 42 V system when the batteries are 'topped off'.

170 V HVDC Bus System

The alternative 170 V high-voltage dc (HVDC) bus system, shown below, does not use the battery bank as the main system bus. The battery bank is connected to only the battery charger and battery converter. Power from sources is converted directly to 170 V dc, and from this bus voltage, the batteries are charged with a charger. Commercial off-line (120 V ac input) switching chargers can also operate on dc of either polarity, and can be used without modification (except for a plug adapter) irrespective of the battery bank voltage.

It might at first seem less efficient, to have to go through a 170 V converter from a power source and then a battery charger to get to the batteries. A direct source-to-battery charger eliminates the inefficiency of the additional source-to-170 V bus converter. However, the HVDC scheme is more efficient when these sources, such as solar power during daylight, provide more power to the load than to the batteries. In the 12 V system, after the batteries are charged, the load power must continue to go through the battery charger(s) to get to the loads. This inefficiency is eliminated in the HVDC system.

Alternative-Energy System

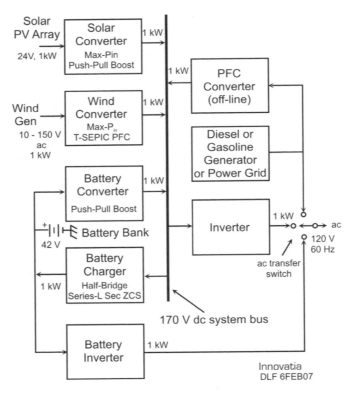

If most of the power use occurs during the day, then for daytime sources such as solar, the HVDC system is more efficient. Energy storage in the battery bank is intended to supply night-time power when the main source is not available, and night power use is usually less for residential electric systems. A system in which the 12 V battery bus is more efficient is one in which light loads are powered by batteries most of the time, with occasional, high-power charging. In this case, charger efficiency is important and the converter for powering the loads less so. But if less power is lost making the source-to-load transfer more efficient than source-to-battery transfer, then the HVDC alternative is best.

HVDC component blocks are functionally somewhat different than for the 12 V system. The inverter component is now only half of what is in a *battery inverter*, which is a combination battery converter followed by an inverter. An existing battery inverter can be adapted to the HVDC system by tapping into its converter output for the HVDC bus. The battery charger can now be a commercial off-line charger. The source converters (solar, wind) will have 170 V dc outputs instead of 12 V or 24 V. The generator source can be converted as easily as with a full-wave rectifier, or more optimally with a power-factor correcting (PFC) dc-dc converter that outputs 170 V. These source converters are what are different in HVDC system components, and their design will be explained to a greater extent in subsequent chapters.

Multiple Bus Sources

In battery-bus systems, ordinarily only one source is permitted to power the rest of the system at any one time. A transfer switch (a 'break-before-make' switch that disconnects from one position before connecting to the other) selects between sources. In the more advanced HVDC system, multiple power sources are allowed to output to the HVDC bus concurrently. How they interact becomes a design consideration. It is possible for a more powerful source to 'crowd out' contributions from lesser sources. As each source regulates its power output to maintain a constant bus voltage, the feedback control loops of the individual sources are affected by what the other sources are doing. Suppose the output voltage is slightly high. How much should a given source reduce its output current? If all sources reduce theirs together, they might share proportionally, though this is not guaranteed. The behavior of a source might also destabilize other sources.

The problem of current sharing among power sources for HVDC bus control is one of prioritization. This reduces to the rule that if solar and wind sources can provide adequate power, they have the priority. Next, the battery converter has priority until it reaches the 'battery low' voltage. The fuel-burning generator then has lowest priority. This scheme can be implemented by placing the decision-making in the battery converter, assuming that it can either start the generator or alert the user for a manual

Off-Grid System Strategy

start and switch-over. The battery converter, however, needs to have as an input the amount of current being contributed by the higher-priority sources. The HVDC bus consequently also includes two other wires which are an input to the battery converter. Each source contributes a small signal current in proportion to its output current on the current sense line (with corresponding ground return); the recommended scale factor is 100 µA/A, or 0.01 % of the output current to the bus. The battery converter terminates the current sense line with an accurate resistor of 1.00 kΩ, 1 %. Then the voltage developed across it is proportional to the total current being sourced to the bus.

The voltage scale factor is $(100 \ \mu A/A) \cdot (1.00 \ k\Omega) = 100 \ mV/A$, with a full-scale sense voltage of 2.00 V for 20 A. This corresponds to a full-scale power of $(170 \ V) \cdot (20 \ A) = 3.4 \ kW$, which can be an intermittent (or 'peak') power value. Ordinary house wiring can be used for the bus power line; 4 mm^2 or # 11 AWG cable is capable of handling 20 A continuously. More typically, 2.5 mm^2 (# 13 AWG) can handle 12 A continuously and 20 A intermittently, and would be the recommended choice for the power wires of the HVDC bus. The third-wire safety ground of electrical cable can also be used to ground the metal enclosures of HVDC components for safety.

With the current-sense wire-pair, not only can the battery converter control its output, each source can also determine the fraction of total current it is supplying. A preferred source can be configured to supply a greater fraction of the total. For instance, solar might be preferred to hydro to preserve the amount of water behind a small dam. The current-sense lines can be implemented as a twisted pair of color-coded 0.50 mm or # 24 AWG insulated wires that run from unit to unit.

The HVDC bus thus consists of two pairs of wires: two color-coded power and two color-coded current sense. With this simple bus, greater optimization and functional capability can be achieved than the established battery-bank bus.

Solar Charger Circuits

For those who are not content merely to buy an existing commercially-available solar charger and live with its performance or who are not satisfied with an existing commercial charger in use and want to be able to repair or improve it, electronic maintenance or design enters the picture. We turn now to some of the considerations in designing your own solar charger or in modifying or maintaining an existing design.

Are Chargers Needed?

Consider first the basic question of why, if 12 V solar panels can be connected directly to 12 V batteries, a solar charger is even needed. If the panels and batteries are matched closely enough so that power transfer is efficient, then a charger would not be needed except to keep the batteries from being overcharged. If the panel power rating (which is its maximum power) is matched well to battery-bank size, then this might not occur, provided that loading stays within narrow limits. As power usage and sunshine vary, battery charge also varies widely and battery life can be reduced. If panel power is limited to prevent overcharging (though occasional, controlled overcharging is needed to equalize cells), then during cloudy times, the batteries might be too deeply discharged. Ordinarily, this is avoided with a backup generator, leaving only the problem of overcharging. Panel sizing should be large enough to overcharge batteries so that on cloudy days, the batteries can still be charged. It depends on whether you want to put your money into panels up-front or into fuel on an ongoing basis.

Solar chargers prevent overcharging and some of them also maximize charging power by matching panels and batteries. They additionally provide an important disconnection of panels from batteries when the panels are not sourcing power. Then the battery bank cannot discharge into the source. A solar charger has some power loss as a power-converting component, though it can save much more than it loses. It can also be low in cost. The Xantrex C-60 60 A charger sold in 2008 for under $200 US.

Solar Charger Enhancement

The Xantrex C-60 charger, shown in 'Solar Chargers and Converters' of *Your own Eco-Electrical Home Power System*, will turn off if it overheats. This can occur if your solar panels are capable of overdriving it. This is a hardy charger design. One has output up to as much as 105 A from a 1.92 kW solar array. Not once have any of the power MOSFETs failed, though the 10 AWG (0.25 mm) wires inside the charger that run across the board from front to rear have gotten so hot that they appear burned from overheating and have unsoldered from their connections to the circuit-board. At over 100 A, one cannot expect a 60 A unit to perform perfectly in all respects.

Solar Charger Circuits

The heat sink mounted at the top of the enclosure, with fins pointing upward, uses convective cooling. However, for overdriven chargers, additional forced-air cooling can be provided by mounting a box fan in front of the unit and operating it from the battery terminals of the charger. Not much air movement is required to make a drastic difference in heat-sink temperature. A simple though adequate fan mount is shown below, with a toggle switch, so that the fan can be turned off when it is not needed, to save power. A couple of insulated 2.5 mm^2 (12 AWG) wires suffice, bent and fed into the mounting holes of the fan with the other ends poked through the holes in the charger front-panel. The 60 mm fan hangs loosely supported by these wires, and the looseness (or compliance) absorbs its vibration.

Xantrex C-60 Circuits

The Xantrex C-60 solar charger is a low-cost, well-designed product, based on a PIC microcomputer (µC). It hardly needs any design refurbishment, other than possibly extending its current output with an additional cooling fan. Occasionally this unit might need to be repaired. Xantrex (formerly Trace Engineering), like Black & Decker (which acquired Vector Mfg.), does not provide circuit diagrams to users and consequently is not an 'open source' company. This is a frustrating policy for home system maintainers. The alternative is to study these products as publicly disclosed by their sale, though it can absorb countless hours.

My tracings of the C-60 circuits, with some explanation, are given as follows. Hopefully, they will be useful for repair and perhaps even for design enhancement. If you neither have nor want a C-60, they are still useful for demonstrating typical low-cost charger circuitry and functions. C-60 circuitry will be presented a fragment at a time. It uses through-hole technology for component assembly. The power circuit consists of four pairs of n-channel power MOSFETs in parallel, as shown below.

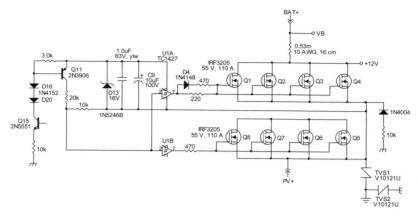

The BAT+ terminal connects to the battery positive terminal as the charger output, and the PV+ node is the solar-panel input. Between them are 8 MOSFETs and a 0.53 mΩ sense resistor consisting of a 10 AWG insulated copper wire about 16 cm long that runs along the side of the circuit-board.

Q1 - Q4 are n-channel MOSFETs connected in parallel. Their 110 A factory ratings are based on near-infinite heat sinking which is rarely found in actual electronic systems. With typical heat sinking, dividing these current ratings by 4 results in workable numbers. Consequently, the four paralleled MOSFETs have a combined current handling capability of about 110 A, well above the 60 A charger rating, but not much above what a large solar array can provide. I have seen as much as 105 A flow through my C-60 and no MOSFET failures have occurred.

The second set of four paralleled MOSFETs, Q5 - Q8, are in series with the first quad but are connected so that the body-drain diodes of the MOSFETs (with cathodes on drains, anodes on sources) are opposed, thereby eliminating any conductive path between input source and battery bank. This is done to prevent battery discharge into solar panels at night, or back into any other source when it is not powering the charger. The +12V node before the sense resistor powers the charger control circuits.

Gate drive to the n-channel MOSFETs requires a voltage that is greater than the voltage at the MOSFET sources by the on-voltage, typically 10 to 15 V. With all 8 MOSFET sources connected together, the same gate supply can be used for the supply of the dual gate driver IC, U1. The gate voltage is at U1A pin 6, and is shunt regulated by zener diode D13, in parallel with storage capacitor C9 and another 1 µF capacitor. The gate voltage, at the cathode of D13, is stacked onto the voltage at the sources and is about 24 V to ground.

The input to the gate drivers of U1 comes from transistors Q15 and Q11. The drive from the µC to Q15 is not shown. When its base is driven high, its emitter voltage follows. For a 5 V drive, the 10 kΩ emitter resistor conducts about 1.7 mA (taking into account the 0.7 V drop across the Q15 base-emitter junction). Enough of this current becomes Q11 base current to turn it on hard and saturate, causing the gate supply

7

Solar Charger Circuits

voltage of about 12 to 15 V to be divided by 20 kΩ and 10 kΩ resistors - a divide-by-3 voltage divider - leaving about 4 to 5 V of drive to the gate driver inputs of U1.

The gate voltage is generated by the circuit shown on the next circuit fragment, below. The gate-drive circuit has been repeated for continuity. Q21, Q22 are a complementary emitter-follower driven by a µC output pin at about 180 kHz with a square-wave (50 % duty ratio). They drive L1, a 100 µH inductor which forms an LC circuit with C26 and the other parallel capacitors at its output node. Together, they have a capacitance of roughly 15 nF and resonate with the inductor at 130 kHz. The inductor output waveform is sinusoidal with a pk-pk voltage of about 20 V. The driver side of the inductor can be seen to clamp above the drive voltage and below ground. (Clamp diodes around the two BJTs are needed but not found on the board.)

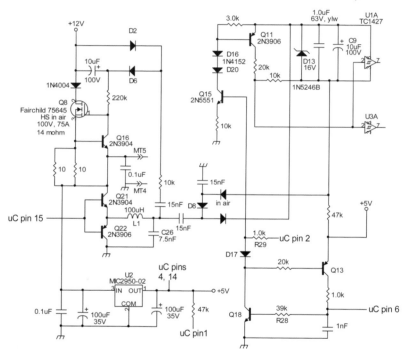

The circuit generates two boosted voltages. The first is for the gate drive of the regulator MOSFET, Q8, through 15 nF, 10 kΩ and D6. When Q22 is on and the output pulled to near ground, the 15 nF capacitor charges through D2 to the sine-wave negative peak. Then when Q21 turns on, its emitter voltage, following the µC pin 15 output level, adds to the voltage across the 15 nF capacitor, and the added voltages charge the 10 µF gate storage capacitor of Q8 to about 25 V to ground.

Q8 and Q16 form a feedback-loop linear regulator with current output determined by the current through the parallel 10 Ω resistors and the base-emitter voltage of Q16. The *b-e* voltage is not the best reference voltage for a stable supply, but it is sufficient to

8

regulate output current to the +5V regulator, U2, and to pin MT5. This is the control power supply for the charger and is about 8.5 V.

Returning to the switching gate supply, two additional 15 nF capacitors along with D8 and associated diodes, form another voltage clamping and stacking circuit. The 'in air' diode that connects to the D8 anode and a 15 nF capacitor to ground lets the capacitor retain its PV+ voltage in the event the array output suddenly drops. This prevents inadequate gate drive and overheated MOSFETs. The low side (anode) of zener diode D13 is connected to PV+, typically 12 V. The circuit works as a voltage doubler, placing 16 V of the zener across C9 for the U1 gate supply.

The gate-driver inputs, from Q11 and Q15, are driven by μC pin 2 which also drives the current-sense circuit, shown below. It PWMs at a frequency of about 160 Hz.

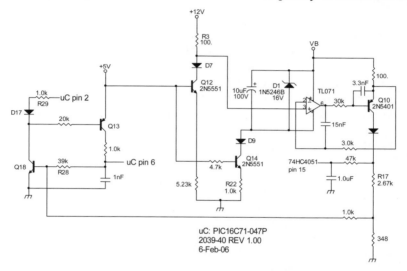

The charging current is sensed as the voltage it drops across the 0.53 mΩ wire resistance. Across this sense resistor are connected two precision 100 Ω resistors of the TL071 op-amp circuit, configured as a voltage-to-current (V/I) converter. A simplified circuit of the V/I converter is shown below.

Solar Charger Circuits

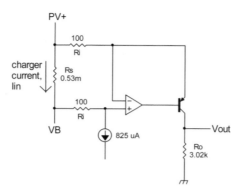

Charger current, I_{in}, develops voltage $I_{in} \cdot R_s = I_{in} \cdot (0.53 \text{ m}\Omega)$ across R_s. The op-amp inverting (−) input voltage, V_-, follows closely the noninverting (+) input, V_+, due to feedback. Then for $V_- = V_+$, the voltage across the upper resistor, $R_i = 100 \ \Omega$, is the same as that across R_s. This voltage replicates a current in R_i that is $R_s \cdot I_{in}/R_i$. A negligible amount of it is diverted to the op-amp input and it flows through the PNP transistor, where it loses a fraction of emitter current to the base, to be sunk by the op-amp output. The remainder is the collector current, calculated from the BJT parameter $\alpha = I_C/I_E$. It develops output voltage, V_{out} across R_o. Then the total transfer function (a transresistance) for this circuit can be written as

$$\frac{V_{out}}{I_{in}} = \alpha \cdot \frac{R_s}{R_i} \cdot R_o \approx (0.995) \cdot \frac{0.53 \cdot 10^{-3} \ \Omega}{100 \ \Omega} \cdot (3.02 \text{ k}\Omega) \approx 16 \text{ m}\Omega$$

For $I_{in} = 60$ A, an output voltage of about 0.955 V results. The 47 kΩ, 1.0 µF RC filter averages it as an input to the µC through the 74HC4051 analog multiplexer at pin 2.

The TL071 is a vintage dual-supply CMOS op-amp. The positive supply pin (7) is attached to VB, the battery. Across its supply pins (7 and 4) are a shunt capacitor and D10, a 16 V zener diode. Both zener and op-amp current is provided by Q14 functioning as a current sink of about 4.3 mA. D9 prevents reverse current whenever VB < 5 V. This floating supply scheme is used to avoid excessive voltage across the op-amp supply terminals when the charger is operated with a 24 V battery-bank.

The TL071 is not 'rail-to-rail' in either its input or output voltage ranges. Consequently, the supply voltages need to be outside the range of the input voltages. The required 'headroom' can be up to 4 V worst-case, though the TI specifications indicate that typically it can operate to the positive supply. R3, a precision 100 Ω resistor, has a voltage drop of about 83 mV across it caused by the Q12 collector current of about 825 µA.

With such small resistances as R_s, it is hard to establish the zero-scale current (0 A) when using low-cost op-amps with input offset-voltage errors of a few millivolts; the

TL071 typically has 3 mV of input-referred error, with a maximum of 10 mV. The full-scale voltage drop across R_s (at 60 A) is 32 mV, only about three times larger than the op-amp input offset-voltage error. At zero-scale, the 82 mV offset causes the output to be nominally 2.5 V, or mid-scale for the μC ADC input.

The μC pins 1, 4, 6, and 14 are part of this circuit. The PIC16C71-047P μC is in an 18-pin DIP package. The pinout, as presented in the Microchip data sheet, is shown below.

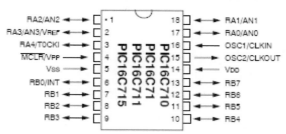

The μC has four ADC inputs (pins 1, 2, 17, and 18). These pins also can function as I/O port bit-lines. Pins 6 - 13 are a byte-wide digital I/O port. Pin 4 is the active-low reset input. The μC is powered from the +5V supply at pin 14. Battery disconnection powers off the charger. The reset line holds the μC in reset until the +5V voltage increases to a logic-high level.

Q18 and Q13 form an overcurrent latch. The 348 Ω, 1 % resistor drops 287 mV from the 825 μA zero-scale offset current. It has a transconductance, with the sensed charging current as input, of 1.835 mΩ, so that the BJT turn-on threshold of about 0.5 V occurs with a current of about 115 A, well above the rated 60 A. This threshold is reasonable for the MOSFETs used. When this current is reached, Q18 turns on causing Q13 to turn on if the μC pin 2 - the PWM source - is not high. Q13 causes the μC pin 6 node - the INT input - to go high, interrupting the μC to warn of overcurrent. It also provides base current through R28 to keep Q18 on. This latched-on state is changed to off only at power-off or when the PWM pin goes high, turning off Q13.

Strangely, the overcurrent latch is not allowed to assert when the power MOSFETs are on! While on, the μC pin 2 PWM level is high, and diode D17 prevents Q13 from turning on, causing latching to occur. At turn-off, however, the output voltage of the V/I converter is held at the overcurrent state by the op-amp 15 nF integrating capacitor. It causes the overcurrent state to change slowly enough that the latch will turn on shortly after PWM turn-off. For the case of the PWM output held high, then the overcurrent circuit is nonfunctional. However, only when PWM is needed to limit the current will overcurrent events arise.

The current-measuring A/D input has a full-scale value of the ADC reference voltage of 5 V. Subtracting the 2.5 V offset, this leaves 2.5 V. Then the full-scale charging current is 2.5 V/16 mΩ ≈ 155 A, well over the current-limit value.

The analog multiplexer and configuration circuitry are shown on the following diagram. The C-60 illustrates minimal-function charger circuitry, with most of the implementation of its function in the μC. The series MOSFET bank is pulse-width

Solar Charger Circuits

modulated (PWMed) to control average charging current during the bulk-charge state. The design presupposes a solar-panel voltage, PV+, which matches the battery-bank voltage and only requires that current be limited. A better charging scheme operates the PV+ source at its maximum input power, to charge at the maximum power produced by the solar array.

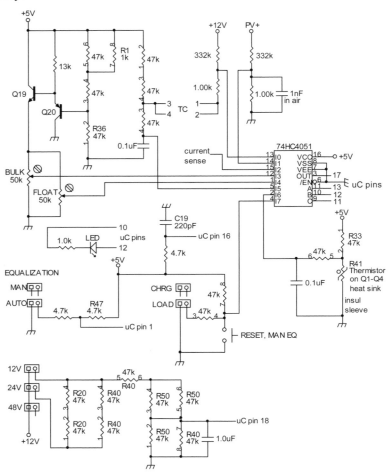

Maximum Input-Power Charging

What is lacking in the Xantrex C-60 is the feature that allows the charger to extract the maximum possible power from the solar array. This function is usually referred to as 'maximum-power-point tracking' (MPPT). It is a control feature that operates a charger so that its effective input resistance matches that of the panel. This results in maximum power transfer.

Maximum Power Transfer

The maximum power transfer theorem is a basic principle of circuit theory. Applied to this problem, it can be stated in reference to the following circuit.

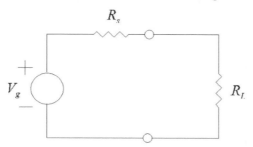

A source is modeled as an ideal voltage source, V_g, in series with an internal resistance of R_s. Maximum power is transferred from the source to the load, R_L, when $R_s = R_L$. When the load is open ($R_L \rightarrow \infty\ \Omega$), no power is transferred to it. When the load is shorted ($R_L = 0\ \Omega$), no power is transferred either. The value of R_L at maximum power must be somewhere in-between these extremes and can be derived. The current is, by Ohm's Law,

$$I = \frac{V_g}{R_s + R_L}$$

The source output power is

$$P_g = V_g \cdot I = \frac{V_g^2}{R_s + R_L}$$

The load power is

$$P_L = I^2 \cdot R_L = \frac{V_g^2 \cdot R_L}{(R_s + R_L)^2} = \frac{V_g^2}{R_s^2 / R_L + 2 \cdot R_s + R_L}$$

The source voltage is fixed at V_g as is R_s, leaving R_L to be varied in the above equation. If $R_L = 0\ \Omega$, $P_L = 0$ W. If R_L is much larger than R_s, then power approaches zero. In the rightmost expression for P_L, power is maximized when the denominator is minimized. This occurs when $R_L = R_s$. Then $P_L = V_g^2 / 4 \cdot R_s$.

Applied to source converters, V_g is the panel open-circuit voltage and R_s is V_g / I_{sc}, where I_{sc} is the panel short-circuit current. For a solar panel, the *incremental* resistance is

Solar Charger Circuits

$\Delta V/\Delta I$ around an operating point. It is not constant but varies with output current and voltage. R_L is the effective resistance of the charger or solar-converter input terminals. For instance, a solar array outputting 24 V and 24 A at maximum power has a resistance, $R_s = 1\ \Omega$. Then the max-P_{in} charger must sink 24 A while maintaining 24 V across its input terminals.

Maximum Input Power Control

Various control schemes can be used to keep the input power at a maximum. From the voltage-current curves for solar panels (for example see companion booklet *Your own Eco-Electrical Home Power System*), the input power curve peaks at the knee of the *v-i* curve. The charger controller must seek this max-P_{in} point of operation.

One simple scheme adjusts the charger converter so that the output current is maximum. For both HVDC and 12 V systems, the output voltage remains nearly constant. If the output current is maximized, and charger efficiency is constant, then the output power is maximum.

Another scheme measures both input voltage and current (which many chargers do anyway), multiplies them in the µC to give P_{in}, and runs an algorithm that maximizes P_{in}.

Either scheme requires that a maximum value be found. What can be controlled is the duty ratio of the charger converter. This controls the average input current. Thus, the input current is varied and P_{in} observed until P_{in} is maximum.

A simple way to find the maximum is to sample at some rate the values of P_{in}, retain the previous value of P_{in}, adjust the input current, sample P_{in} again and compare it with the previous value. If the present value is larger, continue to increase I_{in} until it becomes smaller. Then decrease I_{in}. When the peak of P_{in} has been found, it can be straddled by continuing this procedure. The increments or decrements of I_{in} must be small enough to find the peak and be able to straddle it with sufficient resolution.

Without a µC in a charger, it is more difficult to control max-P_{in}. An analog multiplier which outputs voltage times current followed by a sample-and-hold circuit can retain a previous P_{in} value, and some custom logic in a PAL can sequence the comparison with the present value to iterate the duty ratio. However, all that circuitry is hardly cheaper and more versatile than a small µC.

HVDC Solar Converter

The HVDC solar converter is a battery charger with a 170 V output, not 12 V or 24 V. It is a PWMed dc-dc converter with solar array source of 12 V or 24 V. With output voltage always greater than input voltage, a boost-type converter is most appropriate, though a buck-type with step-up transformer would also work. Engineering evaluation in search of the optimal converter topology has resulted in the *boost push-pull* (BPP) converter topology as the best, shown below.

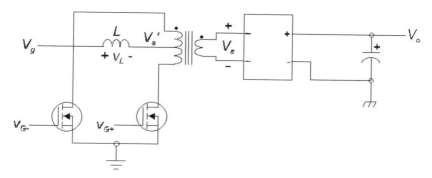

This is a push-pull circuit preceded by a series 'boost' inductor. The secondary circuit is a full-wave diode bridge followed by a storage capacitor. This circuit appears to be optimal from the standpoint of maximizing efficiency and minimizing power component sizing.

Switch sequencing of the MOSFETs for this kind of converter is unusual in that one of the two switches must be on all the time. When both are on, the primary winding of the transformer is shorted and the center-tap is at 0 V. The input voltage, V_g, is applied across the inductor and its current increases for the on-time of $D \cdot T_s$, where D is the *duty ratio* (or duty cycle),

$$D = \frac{t_{on}}{t_{on} + t_{off}} = \frac{t_{on}}{T_s}$$

D is the fraction of the total switching period, T_s, during which a switch is on. The switching frequency is $f_s = 1/T_s$. The inductor current increases during the on-time of $D \cdot T_s$ by

$$\Delta i = \frac{\Delta \lambda}{L} = \frac{V_g \cdot t_{on}}{L} = \frac{V_g \cdot (D \cdot T_s)}{L}$$

where λ is the circuit flux of the inductor; $\lambda = v \cdot t = L \cdot i$, where L is the inductance.

One of the two switches (alternating each half-cycle) then turns off. For the off-time, the fraction of T_s is the complement of D;

$$D' = 1 - D = \frac{t_{off}}{T_s}$$

The primary winding is no longer shorted and the secondary voltage is referred through the transformer *turns ratio*,

Solar Charger Circuits

$$n = \frac{N_p}{N_s}$$

where N_p is the number of primary turns per center-tapped half-winding and N_s is the secondary turns. It appears across each of the primary half-windings as approximately $n \cdot V_o$. (The dots on the transformer windings indicate terminals at the same voltage polarity.) The off switch must be rated to withstand at least $2 \cdot n \cdot V_o$. This voltage must be greater than V_g for inductor flux balance over a switching cycle. The converter waveforms are shown below.

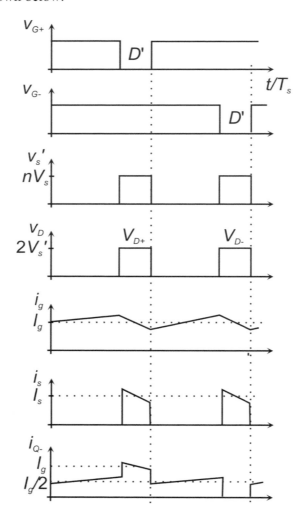

During the off-time of $D' \cdot T_s$, the inductor current decreases by

$$\Delta i = \frac{\Delta \lambda}{L} = \frac{(V_g - n \cdot V_o) \cdot t_{off}}{L} = \frac{(V_g - n \cdot V_o) \cdot (D' \cdot T_s)}{L}$$

Because $n \cdot V_o > V_g$, the change in current during the off-time is negative, or decreasing. For the current waveform to be stable over a switching period, it must have the same values at beginning and end, and the changes must be the same in magnitude. This occurs for a fixed value of inductance when the $\Delta \lambda$ are equal and opposite during on- and off-times. Then

$$\Delta \lambda_{on} = V_g \cdot (D \cdot T_s) = -\Delta \lambda_{off} = (n \cdot V_o - V_g) \cdot (D' \cdot T_s)$$

Canceling the T_s on both sides of the equation and solving for the voltage transfer function of the converter, it is

$$\frac{V_o}{V_g} = \frac{1}{n} \cdot \frac{1}{D'}$$

The voltage transfer function can be thought of as the voltage gain of the converter; V_o is the output voltage and V_g is the input voltage.

The $1/D'$ factor is common to all common-active or 'boost' converters, and the $1/n$ is the transformer voltage gain from primary to secondary windings. Then for $V_g = 12$ V and $V_o = 170$ V, $V_o/V_g = 14.2$.

For this kind of converter, the optimal value of $D' \approx 0.618$. When operated around this value, efficiency is generally highest. We can now calculate n;

$$n = \frac{1}{(V_o / V_g) \cdot D'} = \frac{1}{(14.2) \cdot (0.618)} = 0.1142 = \frac{1}{8.76}$$

Thus the secondary turns should be about 8.8 times that of each half of the primary winding.

The input current waveform of the BPP converter, apart from the current ripple, Δi, is constant. In converter design it is desired to achieve current waveforms for which the rms current is close to the average current value. A design 'figure of demerit' is the *form factor*,

Solar Charger Circuits

$$\kappa = \frac{\text{rms}}{\text{avg}}$$

The resistive power loss in switches and other components varies with the rms value while the amount of current that we want is usually the average. An important goal in design is to make κ as close to one as possible in that $\kappa \geq 1$. For dc or constant current, $\kappa = 1$. The BPP has values of κ for the switches (MOSFETs and secondary-side rectifier diodes) that are lower than other kinds of converters.

In practice, the overlapping gate drive waveforms are not readily produced by commercially available PWM controllers. Control ICs with push-pull outputs can be used if a modification is made to the circuit, by adding a third switch as sketched below. This circuit is easier to implement but does not have as low a κ as the BPP.

The two gate-drive outputs turn on one or the other of the transformer MOSFETs. When both switches are off, the added (middle) boost MOSFET is on. Its gate drive is the logical NOR of the two non-overlapping gate drives. The converter on-time is the off-time of the transformer switches. The transformer switches alternate the current between half-windings when the boost switch is off. The overall converter behavior is the same, yet the added switch allows ordinary PWM controllers with dead-time to be used.

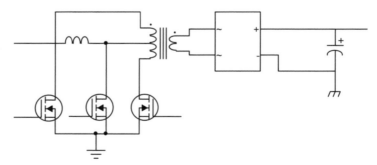

During the delay of about 15 ns through the NOR gate, between when a transformer MOSFET turns off and the boost MOSFET turns on, no switch is conducting the inductor current. For this brief time, this current must still go somewhere. Often, the boost MOSFET drain-source capacitance is large enough to form a resonant circuit with the inductor which charges this capacitance for the brief time the MOSFET is not yet on. If the delay is too long, additional capacitance must be added to prevent the voltage from exceeding the MOSFET rating. The circuit is shown below.

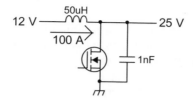

The capacitor energy is dissipated in the boost MOSFET when it turns on, discharging the capacitance. Consequently, the time when all MOSFETs are off must be minimized. The lost power can be calculated from the capacitor voltage, v_C, at MOSFET turn-on and the PWM switching frequency, f_s:

$$P_C = \tfrac{1}{2} \cdot C \cdot v_c^2 \cdot f_s$$

where C is the capacitance. For $C = 500$ pF, $v_C = 35$ V, and $f_s = 100$ kHz, then $P_C = 31$ mW, a negligible loss. The required capacitance size for a maximum v_C can be derived from LC resonance equations. The peak voltage, $\hat{v}$, across L or C of a resonant circuit with peak current, $\hat{i}$, is

$$\hat{v} = Z_n \cdot \hat{i} = \sqrt{\frac{L}{C}} \cdot \hat{i}$$

At MOSFET turn-off, the voltage at the transformer center-tap is

$$V_s' = n \cdot V_s$$

as shown in the converter waveform graphs. The voltage rises as a sine-wave from this voltage with a resonant period of

$$T_n = 2 \cdot \pi \cdot \sqrt{L \cdot C}$$

After a quarter cycle, or $T_n/4$, of ringing the drain voltage peaks at $\hat{v} + V_s'$. After a time of only t_d, the voltage rises to

$$v_C = \sqrt{\frac{L}{C}} \cdot \hat{i} \cdot \sin\left(\frac{t_d}{\sqrt{L \cdot C}}\right) + V_s'$$

19

Solar Charger Circuits

This equation can be used to find the design value of C by iteration; it is not able to be solved using algebra. For an inductor current at turn-off of 100 A, an inductance of 50 μH, a gate delay of 15 ns, $V_s' = 25$ V, and an initial guess for C as 1.5 nF (including the MOSFET $C_o = 500$ pF in parallel), then $v_C = 42.5$ V, a sufficient margin for 55 V MOSFETs. The power loss is $P_C = 179$ mW, an acceptable loss for a 1000 W converter.

The BPP is an appealing converter for both solar and battery converters. Both present low-R_{in} (low voltage, high current) inputs which must be converted to 170 V at much lower currents.

The current transfer function of converters, I_o/I_g, is generally the inverse of V_o/V_g. It has to be for power conservation (at 100 % efficiency), for $V_g \cdot I_g$ must equal $V_o \cdot I_o$. Therefore,

$$\frac{V_o}{V_g} = \frac{I_g}{I_o} = \frac{1}{n} \cdot \frac{1}{D'}$$

For the optimal BPP, $D' = 0.618$ and the previously calculated $n = 1/8.76$, then $I_g/I_o = 14.17$, and with $I_g = 100$ A, $I_o = 7.06$ A. At $V_o = 170$ V, output power is 1.2 kW. This equals the input power of $(12 \text{ V}) \cdot (100 \text{ A}) = 1.2$ kW. Typically, converter efficiency is in the low 90 % range. At 90 %, input power would need to be 1.2 kW/0.9, or 1333 W, and $I_g = 100$ A/0.90 = 111 A.

Battery Inverter Circuits

Commercial inverters designed for off-grid systems are typically much more expensive than low-cost inverters designed to be kept in trucks for occasional use. The inverter coverage in *Your own Eco-Electrical Home Power System* did not cover Xantrex or Outback inverter-charger combinations. The 1500 W units are typically priced around $2000 US each and contain far more electronics than is found in a low-cost unit, such as a Black & Decker (as labeled under Vector Mfg.) VEC050D 1500 W inverter, typically selling for around $250 US. The weight and size differences also are significant. The Xantrex inverter weight is comparable to a bag of cement and is about 3/4 the size. The Vector unit is easily held in one hand and is about the size of a notebook. Why then are these inverters, designed for off-grid use, so different in price, parts-count, weight, and size?

It has in part to do with patents. Once a company has a patent on an idea, it tends to become mired in its invented-here technology. These 'boat anchor' inverters use 60 Hz transformers which are large, heavy, and expensive. They combine transformer outputs to produce a stepped sine-wave, which is better as a sine-wave approximation than a bipolar square-wave. The newer inverter designs, such as those of Vector, are based on switching converter technology with switching frequencies typically around 100 kHz. Some of these converters, such as those sold by Samlex, also output sine-wave approximations of waveforms comparable to the bulky converters.

Another factor in the price difference is the quality of design and components. The low-cost 'portable' inverters, for example, use fans with sleeve or journal bearings, not ball bearings. They are not intended to run every day, day in and day out, and fans will usually be the first component to fail when used continually for home power. However, replacement of these fans with ball-bearing fans is not difficult. As a temporary alternative, fan refurbishment is a feasible home-electric activity. Once a sleeve-bearing fan fails completely, an inventory of the right size of ball-bearing fans should meanwhile have been obtained as replacements.

Fan Repair

Electromechanical components are notorious for shorter life expectancy than electronic parts. Mechanical failure modes are harder to overcome in design. Because of inherent mechanical wear mechanisms, reliable design requires that electromechanical components be specified to account for this fact. However, in an era of cost-driven and time-to-market-driven design, failure-prone electromechanical components appear in power products. Not unique to inverters, the same refurbishment of fans applies to battery chargers and can also apply to other loads such as desktop computers and DVD players.

Battery Inverter Circuits

Repair of box fans is usually simple. The symptom of the most common failure is that the rotor will no longer turn freely because of a worn bearing. Bearing wear is caused by dust, loss of lubricant, and torque ripple, causing the rotor shaft to become grooved. Repair steps are illustrated as follows. A typical cooling fan, this one from a battery charger, is shown below. Most of these fans are now made in Asia, usually by Chinese companies.

The first step is to carefully peel away with a tweezers the round plastic label that covers the access hole to the shaft. Place it somewhere out of the way with the adhesive side up. Its removal exposes the shaft-hole plug, as shown in the next picture. Remove the rubber plug with a small screwdriver blade or tweezers.

Once the plug is removed, the next item to be removed is the plastic C-clip that keeps the shaft from wandering axially in the bearing. It is shown below. Use either a strong tweezers or small needle-nose pliers and a small screwdriver to force the clip from the shaft groove and off the shaft. It will bend, but be careful not to damage the clip.

Next, an optional rubber O-ring might be found under the clip, to seal the shaft. Carefully remove it too. The rotor should now be able to freely move axially and can be pulled out from the stator, as shown below.

Battery Inverter Circuits

Polish the shaft until it is smooth with a light grade of emory cloth, by wrapping a strip of it around the shaft and rotating the shaft until smooth. Wipe the shaft clean with an ordinary cloth or paper towel.

Lubricate the shaft with bearing grease. WD40 or a comparable spray can be used, but I prefer grease, shown in excess on the shaft in the picture below. Be sure to apply plenty of lubricant - however not *this* much.

To reassemble, reverse the disassembly steps.

Fan Driver Redesign

Mechanical maintenance of fans is usually all that needs to be done. However, occasionally an electronics failure occurs. In the fan shown previously, the tan-colored, stator-mounted etched-circuit-board (ECB) can be seen (in the second rotor removal picture) to have four components mounted on it: 2 22 µF electrolytic capacitors, one 1N4007 diode, and a four-terminal IC that was positioned so that the rotor magnets could activate the Hall-effect device (HED) inside it. In the above fan, this component evidently failed. (The other parts tested good.) Rather than attempt to obtain a replacement for an obscure part, I decided to design my own motor-drive, one that I could maintain in the future. Most products have room for a small drive board and the original fan terminal connection provides power for the drive.

The first step in redesign is to characterize the motor. I unsoldered the original red and black power wires connected to the ECB and soldered a three-conductor flat cable to the three motor terminals. One was the center-tap (pin 1) for two opposite-phase windings (pins 2 and 3). Then I connected digital storage oscilloscope (DSO) probes to pins 2 and 3 and the ground clips to pin 1 and spun the rotor with the DSO in normal trigger mode. After a few tries, I captured the following waveforms.

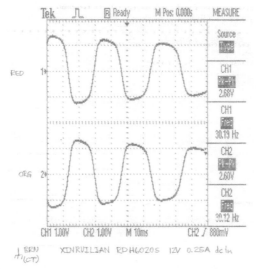

From these waveforms (or extracted measurements of the DSO on the right side of the screen), the *mechanically-referred flux* of the motor (or as motor specifications call it, the 'voltage constant') calculates to be

$$\lambda_{me} = [(2.68 \text{ V}/2)/(30.19 \text{ Hz el})]\cdot 2 \approx [44 \text{ mV/Hz el}]\cdot 2 = 88 \text{ mV/Hz me}$$

The peak induced voltage in the windings by the magnets is about 44 mV per Hz of electrical motor frequency. The mechanical frequency or speed of the rotor is the

25

Battery Inverter Circuits

electrical drive frequency divided by the number of pole-pairs of the motor. The rotor had four poles (count the magnets), making the mechanical frequency half the electrical frequency. With a 12 V supply, the no-load (maximum) motor speed is a fast 135 Hz me, or over 6 krpm - another factor in reduced bearing life.

Note that the two DSO traces show merely an inversion between the waveforms, or 180 degrees of phase difference. I was hoping for a two-phase motor, such as the typical step-motor, for then it is possible to apply drive that produces constant torque with rotor angle. This minimizes torque ripple and the radial component of the torque which causes run-out (mechanical wobble of the shaft) and radial bearing wear. Alas, as is typical in small fans, this is a one-phase motor and a minimum of two phases (forming a two-dimensional plane of rotation) is required to rotate in a plane a drive-current vector referred to the motor magnetic field. With only one phase, the result is a pulsating torque. This torque ripple also wears bearings.

The original fan drive design uses a Hall-Effect Device (HED) rotor position sensor. A magnet edge causes it to advance the drive to apply the correct drive polarity for rotation in a specified direction. I reasoned that for products without a fan filter (such as the battery charger), the direction of air movement is probably not too significant, only that air be moved over heated surfaces. Additionally, I did not want to complicate the redesign by placing position sensors - probably another HED - in the original motor housing. I wanted to minimize wires and bring out only the three winding terminals. Without rotor position sensing, winding-sensed or 'sensorless' phase control is required.

The following one-phase fan-motor drive design spins the motor. Component selection is not too critical. D1, D2 can be anywhere from 1N4002 to 1N4007. The BJTs (Q1, Q2) should be rated for 250 mA, depending on your motor rating. This fan is rated at 12 V, 250 mA and the PN2222 BJTs warm slightly, but not excessively.

The LM393 is a BJT, single-supply, commodity-grade dual comparator. The induced voltage of the windings is sensed by both comparators through an RC differentiator. When the induced voltage at pin 2 of the motor winding goes low, this negative-going edge drives the U1B, pin 6 inverting input, causing the output to be driven active low, turning off Q1. The opposite behavior occurs for U1A and it turns on, driving the motor winding on the right.

C2, R2 and C3, R3 will affect fan drive by affecting how long drive is applied to the motor. The RC time constant affects the comparator input waveform rate of decay. The time-constant is set long enough to provide drive during the entirety of each half-cycle.

Sensorless One-Phase Fan Motor Drive

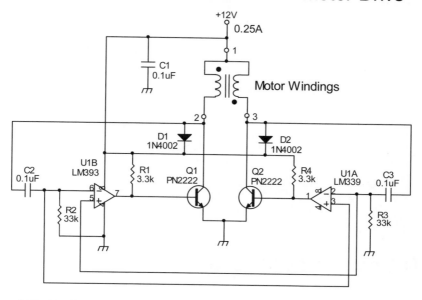

DLF 16SEP07

This simple circuit is symmetrical and no preference is given to starting direction. The fan can spin either way, and on occasion will not start at all. This is unacceptable for a commercial product design, but for a redesign used by a knowledgeable user who manually turns on the inverter, if the fan is not heard to come on, recycle the power. (Then refine the design!) By making the RC time-constants different, the circuit symmetry is changed and the fan might not turn. Driven by this circuit, the fan turns at about 105 Hz el or around 3 krpm. The upper trace, shown below, is at U1, pin 2 and the lower at winding terminal 2.

Box fans used for equipment cooling are not very complicated and not hard to repair or even redesign. The above redesign fits in 1 in^2 (or about 6.5 cm^2) and can be improved without great difficulty. I offer it as a starting point for a design that turns a motor. Hopefully, only bearing reworks will be required to maintain your fans.

Battery Inverter Circuits

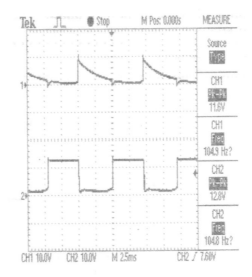

300 W Low-Cost Inverter

We now investigate the characteristics of commercial, low-cost inverters by analyzing an example and assessing what improvements might be made to increase reliability. These low-cost inverters have battery inputs and follow the block diagram shown below.

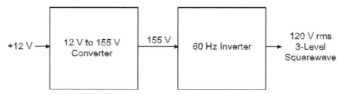

The first low-cost inverter to be examined here has all the telltale signs of East Asian design and manufacture. Optimal electronic design in the developing countries differs somewhat from that of the developed countries because of labor-rate differences. With low labor rates for assembly, it is often better to design using more parts that are lower in cost. Components sourced from the more industrially-developed world are relatively expensive compared to labor. Consequently, it makes sense to use many high-volume 'commodity' parts that are low in cost. The result is *semi-discrete* design: design with less integration but using enduring ('legacy') ICs, such as the SG3525A and TL494 PWM controllers. Parts costing around a penny, such as resistors and diodes, are applied profusely in these designs.

'Item # 40111' inverters with packaging and case are shown below left, with inverter board and side panels removed (at right).

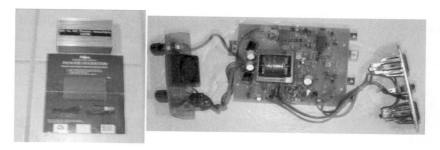

To the left of the board is the input panel, with battery input terminals and attached cooling fan. The two converter power transistors are extending from the left edge under the board. The transformer is that of the converter. The four transistors extending from the right edge of the board are the inverter bridge, with output panel to the right, containing power switch (in middle), two 120 V ac outlets, and power LED next to (below) the power switch. These units cost typically about $50 US in 2008.

Converter Primary Circuit

The converter block consists of the power converter and its controller. The power converter is a *push-pull* circuit, shown below. The transformer has a primary winding center-tap connected to the +12 V supply and a full-wave diode bridge on the secondary.

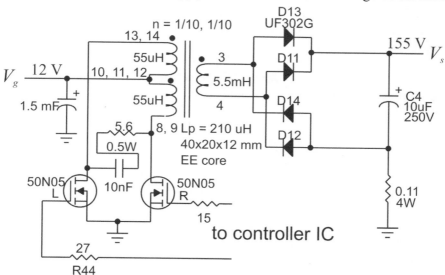

The push-pull circuit is optimal for low-voltage, high-current (low R_{in}) inputs. Only one transistor is in series with the input circuit and the transistors alternate in conducting the primary current. They are in parallel across opposite ends of the primary winding. Because each half of the primary winding conducts for a half-cycle, the power-switch transistors alternately share the current; each conducts on average half the current. A

Battery Inverter Circuits

disadvantage of push-pull is that the utilization of the primary winding is half and the transformer is not used to its full power-handling capability. That is, each half-winding conducts the primary current at most half of the time as they alternate. The secondary winding is fully utilized by using a full-wave rectifier bridge.

The winding dots are used to indicate which ends of the windings have the same voltage polarity. The dotted upper end of the lower half-winding is the positive end of the winding, at +12 V. The lower undotted end is connected to ground (0 V) through R. The dotted end of the secondary winding is the positive end of it, and current will flow out through diode D13 and back into the undotted end through D12. Current into a dotted end is positive.

A pulse-width modulation (PWM) controller drives the gates of the MOSFET switches, labeled L and R. They alternate their switching cycles. Suppose R turns on. Then L is off. Current flows from the input supply, a voltage source of $V_g = 12$ V, into the center-tap and downward through the bottom half-winding, through R to ground, completing the loop back to the V_g supply. With R on, V_g is applied in a positive direction across the bottom winding (dotted end positive) and its flux links with the secondary winding, causing current to flow out of pin 3 (the dotted end) and into pin 4.

When R turns on, it clamps the bottom half of the primary winding across V_g. Because the top half has the same number of turns, the same voltage appears across it and adds to the supply voltage so that the drain voltage of L is $2 \cdot V_g$. Therefore, the MOSFET voltage ratings must exceed twice the input voltage. The drain voltages, v_{DL} and v_{DR}, and other waveforms are shown on the following page. The gate drive waveforms are shown together though only one turns on each half-cycle, as labeled.

When R turns off, the behavior becomes somewhat more complex. Current drops to a small value that transfers to the top half of the winding where it flows in reverse through L and out the center-tap. MOSFETs have a built-in *body-drain diode* through which current can flow in reverse. An equivalent circuit for an n-channel MOSFET is shown below.

If BJTs are used as power switches, then additional shunt diodes must be added to the circuit to conduct the off-time current.

During off-times, only magnetizing current flows in the transformer. The R off-time current is shown in the plot of i_p as positive and decreasing. (It is positive because it flows *into* the dotted end of the top primary winding.) This is the transformer magnetizing current in the primary winding, plotted separately as i_{mp}. The magnetizing current is opposed by V_g which causes it to decrease at the rate of V_g/L_p, where L_p is the half-winding inductance. This inductance is relatively large and the magnetizing current through it decreases slowly.

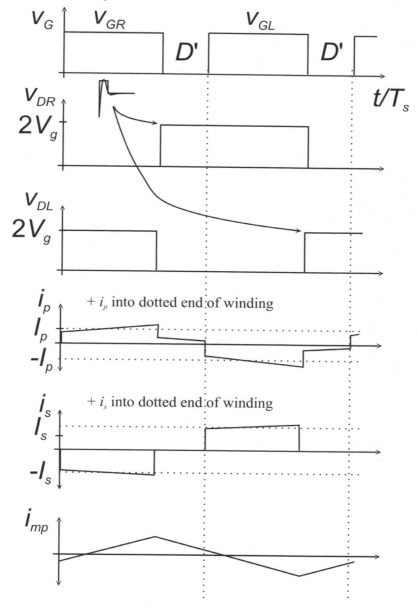

Then L turns on. The voltage across the upper half-winding reverses in polarity. The secondary current resumes and the amount of magnetizing current begins to increase. During the L on-time, most of i_p is transferred to the secondary winding, as $n \cdot I_p$. Both

31

Battery Inverter Circuits

load and magnetizing currents flow out of the dotted end of the top half-winding and are negative in polarity, as shown on the i_p and i_m plots. (i_m continues to be positive for a while until it reverses during the on-time of L.) Though its polarity is negative, i_m increases in magnitude by the rate of V_g/L_p. Each switching cycle is a transformer flux and i_m half-cycle. The peak value of i_{mp} can be calculated from the v-i relationship for inductors;

$$\hat{i}_{mp} = \frac{V_g \cdot T_s}{L_{mp}}$$

The converter PWM controller switches at a frequency of $f_s = 100$ kHz. Then $T_s = 10$ μs and $\hat{i}_{mp} = 2.182$ A.

Leakage Inductance

What complicates turn-off behavior is that primary current does not immediately transfer to the other half-winding because of transformer *leakage inductance*: that part of the winding inductance which does not couple to the secondary winding as magnetizing inductance. The fraction of winding inductance that couples is typically high and is the *coupling coefficient*, k, of the transformer. Typically, $k > 0.99$, and less than 1 % of the winding flux does not couple. Leakage inductance is equivalent to a small external inductance added in series with an ideal transformer. Winding inductance is the leakage inductance, L_l, in series with magnetizing inductance, L_m. For the primary winding,

$$L_p = L_{lp} + L_{mp}$$

The transformer equivalent circuit is shown below, without isolated windings. The secondary circuit is 'viewed' from or *referred* to the primary circuit by transforming secondary voltage as $n \cdot v_s$ and current as i_s/n. Secondary circuit impedances refer to the primary by n^2.

Transformer Equivalent Circuit

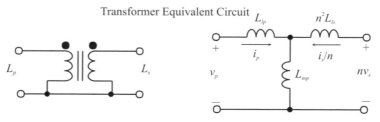

Secondary referred to primary

Transformer primary and secondary windings have only their leakage inductances between them. The magnetizing inductance, L_{mp}, is across both, though from the secondary winding, it will have a value of L_{mp}/n^2. For the transformer of the above circuit with $n = 1/10$, the secondary inductance, $L_s = L_{ms} + L_{ls}$. For $L_{ms} \gg L_{ls}$,

$$L_s \approx \frac{L_{mp}}{n^2} = \frac{55\,\mu\text{H}}{(1/10)^2} = 5.5\,\text{mH}$$

which is the measured value.

Transformer winding currents are of opposite polarity. Current into the dotted end of the primary comes out the dotted end of the secondary while the winding voltages are both positive on the dotted ends. The coupled winding fluxes oppose and cancel, leaving only the uncoupled fluxes of the leakage inductances.

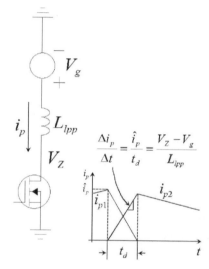

At MOSFET turn-off, immediate transfer of current between primary half-windings does not occur. There is a transition time, t_d, during which current is decreasing quickly in the turned-off winding and increasing quickly in the other windings, as shown, where $i_p = i_{mp}$. In the primary circuit, a voltage opposing the current in the branch that is turning off occurs across $L_{lpp} = 2 \cdot L_{lp}$, the leakage inductance between the two primary half-windings. Then i_p ramps down at the rate of V_p/L_{lpp}.

The primary-generated flux of the shared magnetic path through the ferrite core of the transformer transfers quickly to the other half of the primary winding as it decreases to zero while current increases in the other half-winding. The rate of change of i_p depends on the voltage across the leakage inductance and is

$$\frac{\Delta i_p}{\Delta t} = \frac{\hat{i}_{mp}}{t_d} = \frac{V_Z - V_g}{L_{lpp}}$$

Battery Inverter Circuits

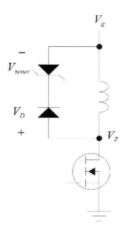

where V_Z is the MOSFET off-voltage. A series zener clamp, as shown here, presents a constant voltage of V_Z at the MOSFET drain. Drain clamp voltage, $V_Z = V_g + V_{zener} + V_D$, where V_D is the diode on-voltage, typically about 0.8 V. V_Z must be limited to the 50 V rating of the MOSFETs (50N05: 50 V, 50 A); let it be 45 V worst-case.

In the plots of v_D above, V_Z is sustained only during the clamping time, t_d, of current transition between windings. After transition is complete, the drain voltage drops to $2 \cdot V_g$.

The delay time can thus be solved from the previous equation;

$$t_d = \frac{\Delta \lambda}{V} = \frac{L_{lpp} \cdot \hat{i}_{mp}}{V_Z - V_g}$$

The wires of the primary half-windings are typically wound together as a *bifilar* winding with high k, typically 0.998 or higher. High k keeps t_d and clamp power loss low.

In this inverter design, as in most, V_Z is determined not by a zener diode but by a series RC snubber. For the given converter, if primary half-winding $k = 0.998$, then by the general formula relating leakage inductance, L_l, to k and winding inductance, L,

$$L_l = (1 - k) \cdot L$$

From the above transformer equivalent circuit, the turns ratio between primary half-windings is one, being bifilar-wound, and the value of L_{lpp} is the series equivalent of the two, or

$$L_{lpp} = 2 \cdot L_{lp} = 2 \cdot (0.002) \cdot (55 \ \mu H) = 220 \ nH$$

For a nominal $V_g = 12$ V, $n = 1/10$, $V_s = V_g/n = 120$ V, then substituting these values into the t_d formula with a worst-case $\hat{i}_{mp} = 2.182$ A, $t_d \approx 7.25$ ns. The switching period, $T_s = 10 \ \mu s$. This is a negligible fraction of T_s. It is a quick rising-edge spike.

At turn-on, the secondary current does not immediately appear either but ramps up quickly through L_{lp} and L_{ls}. Similarly, transfer of magnetizing current between half-windings also has a nonzero transition time.

The voltage across the secondary winding is $V_s = V_g/n$. For $n = 1/10$, then $V_s = n \cdot V_g$ or about 120 V. This is not the labeled 155 V and is low, a deficiency in this design that achieves the rated current but at a low output voltage, closer to the 100 V rms voltage used in Hong Kong. These inverters indeed run at low voltage, presenting to the homesteader the urge to change the turns ratio for a nominal 155 V out. Because the secondary circuit is not isolated from the battery side (typical of low-power, low-cost inverters), 12 additional volts can be obtained by disconnecting the secondary circuit from ground and stacking it onto the fused side of the battery input, resulting in 132 V, a marginal improvement.

Another subtlety during off-time: for either half-cycle, as i_p is decreasing, its flux change causes the secondary winding to have a voltage of V_g/n across it as during on-time. With a full-wave bridge, the diodes conduct, and a fraction of the magnetizing current flows in the secondary. However, referred to the primary, V_s imposes the same voltage across L_m as the primary circuit, and they share magnetizing current in parallel. Ideally, the split is equal, but as the secondary-circuit capacitor is discharged by the load, its voltage becomes slightly less and can divert more of the current from the primary winding. When the other switch turns on, it transfers back to the primary winding.

RC Snubber

At turn-off of MOSFET R, current ceases to increase and the winding voltage polarity reverses, causing the body-drain diode of L to turn on, grounding one end of the snubber. This places the snubber RC in parallel with the parasitic capacitance at the drain node to ground with peak primary current flowing through the lower half of the winding. The v_D waveform detail above shows both a constant, zener-clamped voltage during t_d and also a ringing response of a series RC across the drains. The *RC snubber* forms a resonant circuit with the primary winding leakage inductance. Each primary winding half has a leakage inductance of L_{lp}. In series, the total primary $L_l = L_{lpp} = 2 \cdot L_{lp}$.

Resonances have two parameters of interest, resonant frequency, f_n (or period, $T_n = 1/f_n$), and resonant impedance, Z_n, which is the reactance of L and C each at resonance. MOSFET 50N05 drain-source capacitance plus parasitic transformer capacitance is $C_D \approx 600$ pF. Resonant impedance from L_{lpp} and snubber $C + C_D$ is

$$Z_n = \sqrt{\frac{2 \cdot L_{lp}}{C + C_D}}$$

Without clamping circuitry, what limits the drain voltage when turning off is C_D. In some cases, this is sufficient to limit the drain voltage. The RC snubber is similar in function to the resonant drain-voltage limiting technique used for the boost-push-pull converter in the section, 'HVDC Solar Converter'. The amplitude of the undamped sine-wave can be calculated as the drain magnetizing current at turn-off (which flows in the resonant circuit) times Z_n;

35

Battery Inverter Circuits

$$Z_n = \sqrt{\frac{2 \cdot L_{lp}}{C_D}} = \sqrt{\frac{2 \cdot (110\,\text{nH})}{0.6\,\text{nF}}} = 19.2\,\Omega$$

or

$$\hat{v}_n = \hat{i}_{mp} \cdot Z_n = (2.182\,\text{A}) \cdot (19.2\,\Omega) = 42\,\text{V}$$

Then for maximum battery voltage of 16 V,

$$V_Z = V_g + \hat{v}_n = 16\,\text{V} + 42\,\text{V} = 57\,\text{V}$$

MOSFET voltage breakdown can occur at this voltage if the resonant frequency is high enough to allow the peak of the sine-wave to occur within t_d. The quarter-cycle of sine occurs in $T_n/4$, and in t_d time. Given that

$$T_n = \frac{1}{f_n} = 2 \cdot \pi \cdot \sqrt{2 \cdot L_{lp} \cdot (C + C_D)}$$

then for $C = 0$ nF, $T_n \approx 51.0$ ns and the sine peak is reached in $T_n/4 = 12.76$ ns, within $t_d = 14.5$ ns. For $T_n/4 < t_d$, V_Z will reach a maximum value of

$$V_Z = V_g + \hat{i}_p \cdot (Z_n \cdot \sin(t_d / \sqrt{2 \cdot L_{lp} \cdot (C + C_D)}) + R)$$

The RC snubber provides additional capacitance, which lowers Z_n, increases T_n, and adds resistor damping. Damping eliminates spurious converter oscillations which can generate electrical noise at interfering radio frequencies. The snubber values of 5.6 Ω and 10 nF create a damped series resonance for which

$$Z_n = \sqrt{\frac{2 \cdot L_{lp}}{C + C_D}} = \sqrt{\frac{220\,\text{nH}}{10.6\,\text{nF}}} = 4.56\,\Omega$$

A series resonance is critically damped (that is, is at the onset of ringing) with a series resistance of $2 \cdot Z_n$ or $R \approx 9.1\,\Omega$. For $R = 5.6\,\Omega$, the resonance is slightly underdamped, though winding resistance adds to it. The primary current at turn-off causes a voltage drop across the series resonant circuit resistance of $Z_n + R$. The input-supply center tap of the primary winding causes half the voltage to add to V_g as V_Z. Including the given snubber parts values, then

$$V_Z \cong V_g + \tfrac{1}{2}\cdot \hat{i}_p \cdot (Z_n + R) = 16\,\text{V} + \tfrac{1}{2}\cdot(2.182\,\text{A})\cdot(10.2\,\Omega) = 27\,\text{V}$$

which is below the 50 V MOSFET rating by an adequate margin.
   RC snubber values for critical damping are as follows:

$$C = \frac{2\cdot L_{lp}\cdot \hat{i}_{mp}^{2}}{(V_Z - V_g)^2} - C_D$$

$$R \le 2\cdot Z_n = 2\cdot\sqrt{\frac{2\cdot L_{lp}}{C}} \approx 2\cdot\frac{V_Z - V_g}{\hat{i}_{mp}},\, C \gg C_D$$

If V_Z of 45 V is chosen instead, the 5 % values are: $C = 360$ pF, $R = 47\,\Omega$. Z_n is considerably higher with the smaller C, and so is the margin of MOSFET reliability.
   This push-pull scheme is typical of low-cost inverter products in the 300 W power range. There is no sense resistor from the MOSFET sources to the ground return for sensing and preventing per-cycle overcurrent. The currents are large (33.33 A), requiring small-valued sense resistors which are hard to implement. When they are included, copper wire is often used. Its 0.4 %/°C temperature coefficient (TC) causes the current threshold to be reduced with increased temperature, which can be desirable. Resistance is determined by wire length and conductive area (wire gage).
   If there is an imbalance between the circuits of the two primary winding halves, then it is possible for magnetizing current to increase, cycle by cycle, 'ratcheting' upward without restraint until a MOSFET fails. This can occur from flux imbalance between the halves caused by unequal inductances or on-times. If the change in flux of the half-cycles - the on-voltage times the on-time - are not quite equal, the net current for the full switching cycle is not quite zero. For each successive cycle, the net current increases in the direction of the half with the greater flux.
   There is no control of transformer magnetizing current in a voltage-driven circuit like this, and i_{mp} runaway can occur. Series resistance opposes it in that the side with the higher flux conducts more current, a greater voltage drop occurs across its winding and the MOSFET on-resistance, and its flux-generating voltage (and hence flux) is reduced. Circuit resistance, however, is intentionally kept low in transformers to keep electrical power loss low. With a sense resistor and *overcurrent protection* (OCP) circuit, failure from flux runaway can be avoided. A better approach is to not use this circuit but add an input series inductor and control for a BPP converter, as described in 'HVDC Solar

Battery Inverter Circuits

Converter' of the previous chapter. The series inductor dominates over winding inductances and maintains a controlled current.

Push-Pull Converter Currents

The fraction of a switching cycle for either L or R is the duty-ratio, D, which is varied by the controller. D remains the same (or very nearly so) for both half-cycles. By varying D the cycle-averaged voltage and current are varied. For greater output voltage, D is increased.

The current input from the supply, i_g, is the sum of the upper and lower primary half-winding currents:

$$i_g = i_U + i_L$$

The average primary winding current is the same for each half-winding.

$$\bar{i}_p = \bar{i}_U = \bar{i}_L = \tfrac{1}{2} \cdot D \cdot I_p = \tfrac{1}{2} \cdot \bar{i}_g = \bar{i}_Q$$

The bar above the symbol indicates 'average'. I_p is the amplitude of the primary current in a half-winding during the on-time. This current does not stay constant because of changing i_{mp}, but i_{mp} is usually small and to simplify calculations, it can often be excluded without serious inaccuracy. This simplification is called the *small-ripple approximation*. Consequently, we take I_p and I_s to be constant at the average values of i_p and i_s during on-time, as shown in the previous converter waveform plots.

The average input current is $\bar{i}_g$, and $\bar{i}_Q$ is the average switch current (where Q denotes a transistor). The average input current for a 300 W inverter must be nominally (300 W)/(12 V) = 25 A. The form factor (see 'HVDC Solar Converter' section) is lowest (as desired) when duty-ratio, D, is high. For $D = 0.75$ (which gives a ±25 % range on V_g), then the on-time primary current, I_p, will be, on average, about 25 A/0.75 = 33.33 A in amplitude.

Power transistors are rated by their rms currents, for that is the value of the current that relates to their power dissipation;

$$\bar{P}_Q = \tilde{i}_D^{\,2} \cdot r_{on}$$

The rms currents are

$$\tilde{i}_{QU} = \tilde{i}_{QL} = \tilde{i}_Q = \tilde{i}_p = \sqrt{\tfrac{1}{2} \cdot D} \cdot I_p = \bar{i}_g / \sqrt{2 \cdot D}$$

The ½ is from the alternating cycles of drive. The on-time amplitude is

$$I_p = \tilde{i}_g / \sqrt{D}$$

For the secondary circuit,

$$\bar{i}_s = D \cdot I_s \; ; \tilde{i}_s = \sqrt{D} \cdot I_s \; ; I_s = n \cdot I_p$$

The diodes conduct for a magnetic half-cycle each and like the active (transistor) switches, have reduced currents of

$$\tilde{i}_D = \sqrt{\tfrac{1}{2} \cdot D} \cdot I_s$$

The form factors for currents are

$$\kappa_g = \frac{1}{\sqrt{D}} \; ; \kappa_Q = \kappa_p = \frac{\tilde{i}_p}{\bar{i}_p} = \sqrt{\frac{2}{D}} \; ; \kappa_s = \frac{\sqrt{D}}{D} = \frac{1}{\sqrt{D}} \; ; \kappa_D = \kappa_Q$$

The voltage and current transfer function is

$$\frac{\bar{v}_s}{\bar{v}_p} = \frac{\bar{i}_p}{\bar{i}_s} = \frac{1}{n} \cdot D$$

Power Supply and Protection Circuits

The control supply has some protection functions, as shown below. The automotive blade fuse is a typical feature of low-cost inverters. This one is conveniently located on the input panel for easy replacement. It is followed by four electrolytic capacitors which provide a local, low-impedance source of dynamic current to the converter.

The body-drain diodes of the L and R MOSFETs will conduct if a negative (reverse) voltage is applied to the battery input, thereby blowing the fuse, if not first the MOSFETs themselves. The transformer winding inductance helps to keep the current from rising too fast, though at 55 μH per side, it probably will not limit the current rise sufficiently to give the fuse time to blow. With both MOSFET diodes conducting through coupled primary windings, winding fluxes aid and quadruple inductance. Even so, 12 V/220 μH is about 55 A/μs, too fast for the fuse to blow in time. The single worst

39

Battery Inverter Circuits

act of abuse to an inverter is to swap the battery terminals. They could be protected by design with a high-current series diode, but the resulting decrease in efficiency works against it, the diode cost is avoided, and caution is advised instead.

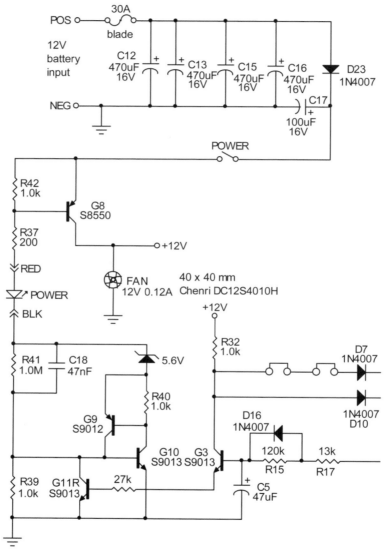

The power switch powers the control circuitry, in this case through an active PNP switch, G8. The +12V supply is not regulated, though a large lead-acid battery is usually a sufficiently good voltage source. Diode D22 prevents damage to the switched circuitry in the event of battery polarity reversal. The fan runs whenever power is switched on.

The +12V BJT, G8, will not conduct unless it has adequate base current, supplied by the series components to ground, beginning with R37 and the output-panel POWER LED. R41 and R39 complete the path to ground, though the high value of R41 (1.0 MΩ) will prevent G8 from conducting sufficiently to power the +12V supply. The right branch must also conduct, through a 5.6 V zener diode and two BJTs configured as a discrete SCR latch.

When power is switched on, a transient of current through C18 will cause the voltage across R39 to rise and turn on G10. It conducts, dropping voltage across R40, and G9 turns on, providing base current back to G10, keeping it on. This is the latch behavior. The latch BJTs will not conduct, however, unless the voltage at the LED cathode is at least 5.6 V - enough to turn on the series zener. Actually, more voltage than this is needed. We can calculate the minimum voltage by working upward from the latch BJTs. When they are on, their *b-e* junction voltages of about 0.65 V each add to the 5.6 V zener, giving 6.9 V. If the LED drops the usual 1.2 V, then the voltage at the bottom of R37 must be 8.1 V. The control circuits will not be powered without at least 8.1 V input. This is an intentional *undervoltage protection* (UVP) scheme. It is needed to keep MOSFETs from being underdriven. If MOSFETs do not have sufficient gate voltage, they only partially turn on, have high resistance, dissipate excessive power, and fail. The UVP circuit prevents any gate drive from being applied to the MOSFETs by assuring that the input voltage is sufficient to drive them. According to this design, 8.1 V is sufficient, and this agrees with the 50N03 manufacturer's data.

From the other end of the series start-up branch, with a nominal 12 V battery, there are two diode drops - D23 and G8 *b-e* - placing 10.7 V on the top end of R37. Then the current through R37 is (10.7 V − 8.1 V)/200 Ω = 13 mA.

If G11R is on, G10 is turned off by it and the latch turns off. This turns off the +12V supply, powering down MOSFET drive circuits. G11R is driven by G3. It in turn is driven by a comparator that performs *overcurrent protection* (OCP) of the inverter.

Converter Control

The converter circuit of the 300 W inverter is shown below.

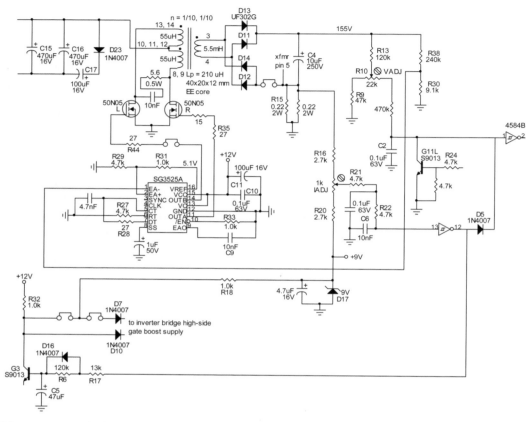

The power switches are driven by a SG3525A pulse-width modulator (PWM) control IC. In this circuit, it has a PWM frequency of nominally 100 kHz, or a switching period, $T_s = 10$ μs, with a dead-time, $t_d = 0.7$ μs. The full magnetic push-pull cycle frequency is half, or 50 kHz. L and R each drive the transformer for a half magnetic cycle and a full PWM cycle. The maximum Δi_{pm} in the primary winding is now calculated more accurately as

$$\Delta i_{pm} \leq \frac{v_p \cdot \Delta t}{L_p} = \frac{12\ \text{V} \cdot 9.3\ \mu s}{55\ \mu\text{H}} \cong 2\ \text{A}$$

or about 7.5 % of the total current, a not unreasonable value. As noted previously, any flux asymmetry between the two primary half-cycles can cause a ratcheting magnetizing current that has nothing to limit it. This is a potential cause of failure for a voltage-controlled PWM loop. But this loop is controlled somewhat differently, as we will see.

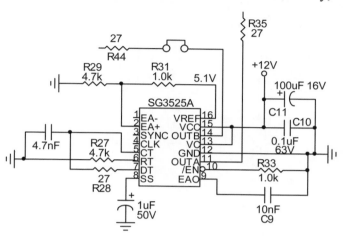

The converter control circuit, shown above, has a SG3525A controller IC. Its block diagram, with design data notes, is given below. The oscillator generates the PWM frequency, based on timing components C_T and R_T. For $C_T = 1$ nF, some corresponding values of R_T and on-times are given in the following table.

R_T, kΩ	t_{on}, μs
6.2	5
10	8
12	10
16	12
20	15
33	20
51	40
68	50
2 kΩ, 470 pF $\rightarrow$ 400 kHz	
200 kΩ, 0.1 μF $\rightarrow$ 120 Hz	

Battery Inverter Circuits

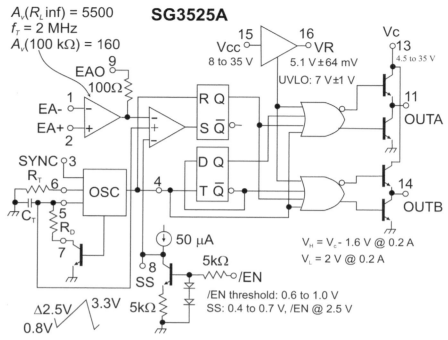

The off-time is calculated as

$$t_{off} = 450 \text{ ns} + (4 \text{ ns}/\Omega) \cdot R_D$$

Then for $R_D = 100 \ \Omega$ and $39 \ \Omega$,

$$t_{off}(100 \ \Omega) = 0.7 \ \mu s \ ; \ t_{off}(39 \ \Omega) = 0.5 \ \mu s$$

Output voltage regulation by the SG3525A is based on nonlinear loop behavior. R38 and R30 of the converter diagram form a voltage divider of × 1/27.37. The divided voltage is input to the inverting error op-amp. The non-inverting input is set at 4.205 V by the R31, R29 divider from the reference voltage of 5.1 V at pin 16. The op-amp output has no feedback to the input except a 10 nF C (C9) to ground, making the loop gain large. (The board layout has a 'C8' screen-printed and connected between pins 1 and 9, but without a part inserted.) Error amplifier detail is shown in the following diagram. The error op-amp functions essentially as an integrator.

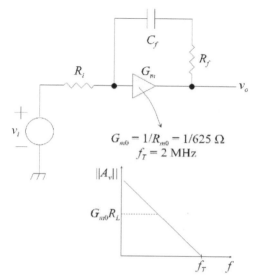

$$G_{m0} = 1/R_{m0} = 1/625\ \Omega$$
$$f_T = 2\ \text{MHz}$$

From the divider calculations, an output voltage of ≥ 115 V will flip the error op-amp output low, turning off PWMing. The output thus has an unavoidable ripple superimposed upon it.

No attempt is made to stabilize the converter control loop. This circuit controls using bursts of PWM cycles of varying D so as to make the output voltage average to around 115 V rms. Even this voltage is low in that the inverter D must be essentially 100 % for an rms voltage of 115 V.

Converter Secondary Circuit

The transformer secondary winding inductance was measured to be 5.5 mH, inferring a turns ratio of $N_p/N_s = 1/5$, where the primary winding is end-to-end (across $2 \times 55\ \mu\text{H}$). Then the secondary voltage is ten times the applied primary voltage of about 12 V (minus circuit drops) or 120 V dc. This is a rather low voltage, requiring higher inverter D to achieve 120 V rms, and consequently higher conduction loss.

The secondary-winding diodes, D11 through D14, are fast recovery diodes that look like the 3 A size. The secondary circuit returns to ground through a sense resistance (R16) of 2 paralleled 0.22 Ω, 2 W resistors. The voltage at the winding-connected side will be negative. At the overcurrent threshold, the voltage at pin 13 of the Schmitt-input inverter will be reduced to where the output will go high. The voltage is offset through a current adjustment pot in a divider that raises the current-sense voltage from a +9 V supply, derived from zener D17 at the top-middle of the diagram. A two-stage low-pass filter and $\times\ \frac{1}{2}$ divider (R21, R22, R26, C6 and a 0.1 μF C) averages the sensed current, making overcurrent protection useless for fast impulses that can destroy both converter and inverter transistors.

Battery Inverter Circuits

The Thevenin equivalent circuit of the I ADJ divider at the wiper of the trim-pot is 4.5 V behind 1.65 kΩ. The voltage at the pin 13 input is thus 4.5 V. The V_{DD} of the hex inverter IC is 9 V, and the thresholds are at 46 % and 53 % of V_{DD} (for $V_{DD} = 10$ V, 25 C), and they vary strongly with temperature and V_{DD}. Thus, the current limit threshold is roughly around 4.14 V. The attenuation from current-sense resistor to pin 13 is the same as the 9 V supply, or 0.5. For a change in voltage of $(4.5 - 4.14)$ V $= 0.36$ V at pin 13, the sensed voltage must change by 0.72 V, corresponding to a current of 0.72 V/0.11 Ω $= 6.5$ A.

Inverter Circuit

The inverter stage is a full-wave MOSFET bridge driven by a 60 Hz clock generator. Average (not peak per-cycle) load overcurrent protection is effected by an average current limiter circuit. The inverter stage also has duty-ratio compensation for converter output voltage.

The output waveform is not sinusoidal but is a three-level square-wave as shown on page 9. The switching period, $T_s = 1/60$ Hz $= 16.67$ ms, and the duty ratio (or duty cycle), D, is adjusted so that the rms value is 120 V. The rms value of a square-wave is

$$\tilde{v} = \hat{v} \cdot \sqrt{D}$$

where $\hat{v}$ is the peak voltage. Then for a given rms value, solving for D, the duty ratio is

$$D = \left(\frac{\tilde{v}}{\hat{v}}\right)^2 = \frac{1}{(\hat{v}/\tilde{v})^2} = \frac{1}{(\text{crest factor})^2}$$

A sine-wave of 120 V rms has a peak voltage of

$$\hat{v} = \sqrt{2} \cdot \tilde{v} \cong 1.414 \cdot \tilde{v} = 1.414 \cdot 120 \text{ V} \cong 170 \text{ V}$$

Then for a bipolar square-wave of the same peak voltage,

$$D = \left(\frac{\tilde{v}}{\sqrt{2} \cdot \tilde{v}}\right)^2 = \left(\frac{120 \text{ V}}{170 \text{ V}}\right)^2 = \frac{1}{2} = 0.5$$

The converters of some low-cost inverters output less than 170 V; 155 V is a typical value. For them,

$$D = \left(\frac{120 \text{ V}}{155 \text{ V}}\right)^2 = 0.6$$

To compensate for variations in converter output voltage, some inverters adjust D to keep the rms value constant.

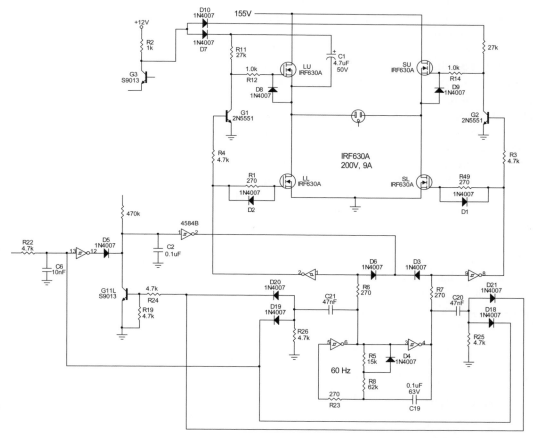

The inverter-stage circuit is shown above. The four H-bridge MOSFETs of the inverter are rated 200 V, 9 A (IRF630), and they drive the output socket terminals directly. The high-side gate supply circuit consists of C1, C3, which store the gate-drive charge, and D7, D10, which charge them from +12V through R2. When the L or S output terminals are low, C1 or C3 charge through the series diode to about 11 V. Diodes D8, D9 protect from gate-source overvoltage when the high-side MOSFETs are driven off.

High-side translator transistors G1, G2 drive the high-side gates, and slowly, with 27 kΩ pull-up resistors and 1.0 kΩ series gate resistors. The passive pull-up resistors make high-side turn-on slower than high-side turn-off, and low-side turn-off is sped by D1, D2 across the low-side series gate resistors. Fast turn-off and slow turn-on avoids conduction overlap, or *shoot-through*, of high- and low-side switches on the same side of the H-bridge. Overall, this is a typical, discrete H-bridge driver scheme.

Another possible failure mode in the H-bridge is high-side MOSFET over-temperature failure caused by gate supply undervoltage. This might occur when the gate source is switched off by G3 during over-current. Whether a cause of failure exists is not immediately deducible from the circuit diagram; more study is needed to be sure gate-supply switching will always result in reliable behavior.

The bridge inputs are driven by 4584B inverters (pin 4, 6 out). They are driven by the 60 Hz oscillator, consisting of inverters with output pins 8 and 10. The square-waves on these pins are inverted relative to each other. The oscillator outputs also drive C20, C21, which form an RC differentiator with R25, R26 and drive a pair of diode OR gates. The D18, D19 gate stores the differentiated voltage edges of the oscillator transitions on C6, at overcurrent inverter input pin 13. The purpose of this is apparently to reset the overcurrent Schmitt inverter during overcurrent conditions. D5 turns off the bridge during overcurrent (pin 12 high).

The other diode OR gate, D20, D21, pulses on transistor G11L each half-cycle. This BJT resets the voltage ramp (or exponential) on C2, as it is charged by the V ADJ network including R9, R10, and R13. As the converter output voltage increases, the ramp slope increases, causing the pin 1 input inverter to output a low level earlier in the cycle, shortening the on time and decreasing D. The bridge drive is gated off through another diode pair, D6, D3. The relationship between converter voltage - which is essentially the peak output voltage - and D is inversely proportional, while the relationship for exact compensation is by the square-root. The linear compensation provides a first-order correction for relatively small changes in peak voltage.

The inverter H-bridge directly drives the output. Power line transient loading or reactive surges are directly applied to it. An LC filter between the output and H-bridge could reduce failures due to line events and also attenuate the high-frequency components of the output square-wave. It would also increase the cost.

Improvement Possibilities

Analysis of the 300 W inverter has revealed several weaknesses in the design:
1. No per-cycle current limit for the converter switches.
2. No converter flux imbalance correction for the push-pull stage.
3. PWM burst control of converter results in output ripple and noise. Linear control would be better, with a converter inductor.
4. Peak voltage at converter output too low to be optimal, causing excessive D and conduction loss in inverter.
5. Inverter overcurrent detection too slow (averaged) and inaccurate for high-current transients.

6. High-side gate supply leaves H-bridge with possibly inadequate undervoltage protection.
7. Inverter outputs high frequencies and has a lack of protection against load-caused events.

Comparison of this inverter with a comparable inverter, the VEC034 shown below, reveals some differences. The VEC034 increases the secondary voltage by returning the ground side of the secondary circuit to the top of the battery input, adding a nominal 12 V without an increase in converter part size. This scheme is inherently non-isolating, having a common ground between battery and ac outlet circuits, and can be used only in low-power inverters. The same converter control IC is used, with an additional LM324 to perform overtemperature, undervoltage, overvoltage, and warning-buzzer driver functions. The output voltage regulation uses divider feedback, though the converter is a 'chopper', lacking a converter inductor for current control. An additional inductor in the secondary circuit would make the converter a push-pull buck ('Buck Converter Circuit', p. 85) with $V_o/V_g = D$, and linear feedback-loop control would be possible. Alas, an additional magnetic device would cost too much, make the package larger, not be absolutely essential, and is consequently omitted.

Battery Inverter Circuits

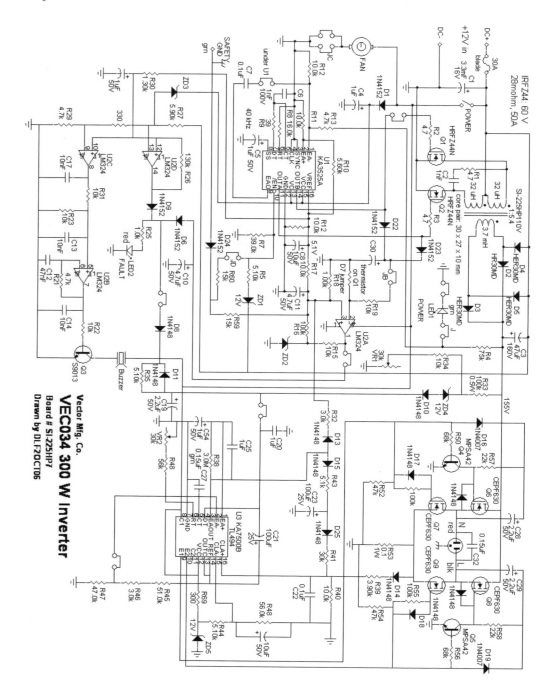

Vector Mfg. Co.
VEC034 300 W Inverter
Board # SI-225HP7
Drawn by DLF2OCT06

The VEC034 does something else that is clever. The push-pull gate drives are diode ORed by D22, D23 and filtered, resulting in an average voltage proportional to the on-time or *D*. This voltage is the source for a thermistor temperature-sensing voltage divider, the output of which (U2A, pin 2) is compared with the divided reference voltage. This scheme adjusts the temperature threshold at which overcurrent protection activates by reducing the threshold temperature as the transistors are driven harder (longer on-time). This effectively is a *feedforward* speed-up of thermal protection.

The VEC034 has a very similar inverter stage, though the driver for it that generates 60 Hz is another PWM controller IC, the TL494 (or the Samsung KA7500). The inverter H-bridge has a low-side sense resistor for overcurrent protection from overload. Its voltage is input to one of the two TL494 error amplifiers. VR2 adjusts the output frequency.

The JWIN JA-D200W inverter, shown below, has converter circuitry similar to the VEC034 but generates inverter waveforms using discrete logic parts.

JWIN JA-200W Inverter Generator

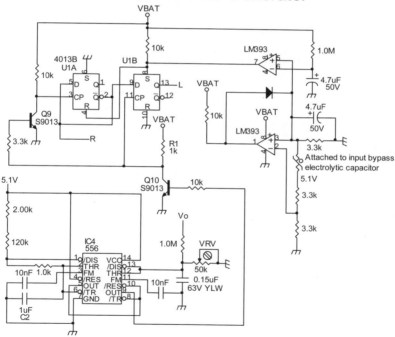

The 556 is a dual 555 timer, shown below. The left-side timer generates a square-wave of 120 Hz frequency. C2 charges through the three series resistors totaling 123 kΩ. When the threshold voltage, 2/3 VCC, of the THR-input comparator is reached, the output goes low. Then /DIS, an open-collector output, pulls low and discharges C2 through the 1.0 kΩ resistor. When the C2 voltage goes below the /TR threshold of VCC/3, the timer RS flop is triggered, /DIS turns off and OUT goes high.

Battery Inverter Circuits

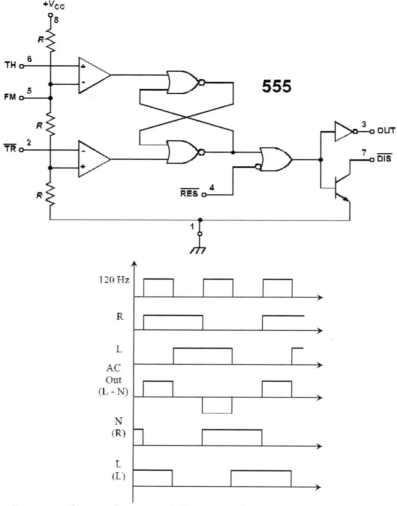

The pin 5 output triggers the second timer, configured as a monostable multivibrator (MMV) or 'one-shot'. When triggered, its pin 9 OUT goes high and the 0.15 µF timing capacitor is charged by the converter output voltage, V_O, which is the inverter H-bridge input voltage and the square-wave peak voltage. As it increases, more timing current flows through the 1.0 MΩ resistor and the THR voltage is reached sooner. This pulse duration sets the bridge on-time and the effect of V_O on timing is an approximate compensation of D to keep the rms voltage constant.

The CMOS 4000-series dual D flops output the bridge drive waveforms, L and R, for each side of the H-bridge. When the timer pin-9 output goes high, the output of Q9 is a rising edge that toggles U1A. As a divide-by-2 flop, it outputs a square-wave on pin 2 that sets up the D input to U1B. When the timer output falls, U1B is clocked. The generated waveforms are shown.

VEC050D 1500 W Battery Inverter

For higher power output, such as 1 kW or more, battery converter components do not simply grow larger in size. Smaller inverters of about 350 W are paralleled. Sometimes this is done by placing the secondary windings of the individual converter stages in both series and parallel. If two secondary windings are placed in series, then each need only output half the voltage. The turns ratio is then doubled as is the output current. Power is still conserved, but the output supply is shared by stacking voltages at double the current. Alternatively, secondaries that output the correct voltage are placed in parallel. Both series and parallel converters are found in inverters such as the Vector Mfg. VEC050D. A top view of its circuit-board is shown below.

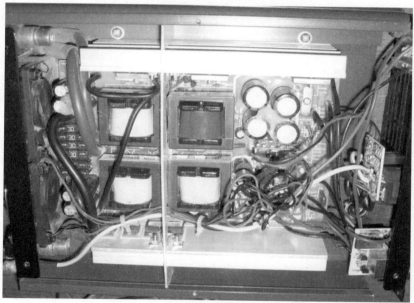

Magnetic cores are commercially available up to the EC70, with a volume of 39.6 cm^3 and capable of handling 3 kW at 175 kHz. Yet these large cores are not usually found in 3 kW switching converters. There is an optimal converter size of around 350 W. As transformer size increases, the magnetic material volume in which core power loss occurs increases more quickly than surface area. For a simple shape such as a sphere the surface area is

$$A_{sphere} = 4 \cdot \pi \cdot r^2$$

Battery Inverter Circuits

while the volume is

$$V_{sphere} = \frac{4}{3} \cdot \pi \cdot r^3$$

As sphere radius increases, the volume increases faster than the surface area. The power loss in the core at a given power-loss density increases with volume; the heat removal increases with surface area. It is easier to 'get the heat out' of a smaller volume and the power-loss density in smaller cores can be made larger. Thus, too large of a core is inefficient. Yet if converter cores are too small, a large number of converters and parts is suboptimal. The many converter fixed power losses also increase inefficiency. The optimum core size seems to be around ETD29, ETD34, or ETD39 cores in the 200 to 500 W range.

The Vector Mfg. VEC050D battery inverter is rated at 1.5 kW and has four ferrite EI-core 40 × 35 × 10 mm E40 transformers, capable of handling 250 W at 100 kHz with a core loss density of about 100 mW/cm³. The turns ratio, with primary turns that of a half-winding, is 3; 12 V drive on the primary ($V_p = 12$ V) results in $V_s = 36$ V. One transformer (taped blue) has an additional control-supply winding for the inverter side of the isolated converter, a push-pull 'chopper'. The primary windings are four strands of what appear to be # 20 AWG magnet wire, having an rms current capability of about 9.3 A, an inductance of 22 µH (per half-winding), and less than 10 mΩ of resistance at 1 kHz. Because of the skin effect, the resistance (not reactance) varies with frequency. Many RLC meters measure with a 1 kHz sine-wave, as a standard frequency for measuring wire resistance. The coupling coefficient is measured to be $k \approx 0.9975$.

Battery Converter Power Equations

At the 3 kW peak rating, the input current from the battery is a nominal 3 kW/12 V or 250 A. Six 30 A automotive blade fuses are paralleled at the input for 180 A total. Eight 2.2 mF electrolytic capacitors on the fused side of the input terminals supply the peak transient current. (The boost push-pull converter, though adding an input inductor, would eliminate this large capacitor bank; see 'HVDC Solar Converter', p. 18.) Push-pull chopper input current is

$$i_g = i_U + i_L$$

where U and L refer to the upper and lower primary winding halves. Their currents are those of the transistors, both rated by rms currents:

$$\tilde{i}_Q = \tilde{i}_p = I_p \cdot \sqrt{\frac{D}{2}} = \frac{\bar{i}_g}{\sqrt{2 \cdot D}}$$

54

where I_p is the average amplitude of the on-time primary current waveform,

$$I_p = \frac{\overline{i_g}}{D} = \frac{\widetilde{i_g}}{\sqrt{D}}$$

Both half-cycles of switching result in input current and for i_g,

$$\widetilde{i_g} = \sqrt{D} \cdot I_p$$

The average primary current is

$$\overline{i_p} = \overline{i_Q} = \frac{D}{2} \cdot I_p = \frac{\overline{i_g}}{2}$$

The secondary currents are

$$\overline{i_s} = D \cdot I_s \; ; \widetilde{i_s} = \sqrt{D} \cdot I_s$$

with transformer turns ratio, n, setting the on-time current amplitude;

$$I_s = n \cdot I_p$$

Using these equations and the ratings, the maximum average input current occurs at the minimum battery voltage of 10.5 V and is

$$\overline{i_g} \leq \frac{\overline{P_g}}{V_g(\min)} = \frac{1500 \text{ W}}{10.5 \text{ V}} = 143 \text{ A}$$

Push-pull converters operate optimally (minimum κ; see p. 21) at high D. For a battery voltage range of 10.5 V to 14 V, the nominal 12 V value of D for a minimum D of 0.95 is $0.95 - (1.5 \text{ V}/12 \text{ V}) = 0.825$, and for 14 V in, the minimum D is $0.95 - 2 \cdot (1.5 \text{ V}/12 \text{ V}) = 0.7$. Over the range of D,

Battery Inverter Circuits

$$I_p = \frac{\bar{i}_g}{D} = 153\ \text{A}$$

Hence, the 180 A fusing using 30 A fuses is correct.

Converter Voltage Feedback Circuit

VEC050D Converter Voltage Feedback Circuit

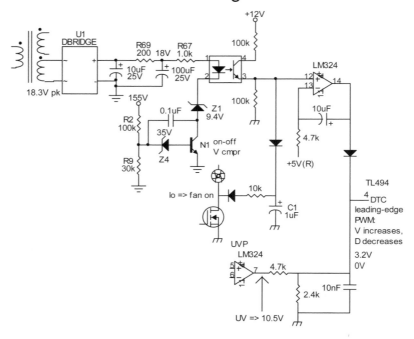

In high-power battery inverters, the input and output are isolated. This results in the use of an optoisolator, to feed back the converter output voltage for regulation. The somewhat simplified feedback circuit is shown above.

The VEC050D uses a TL494 PWM controller. It has a 'dead-time control' or DTC pin which functions as an inverting or leading-edge modulator input; as the DTC voltage increases, D decreases. The output-side control supply winding of 18.3 V peak is filtered and applied to the LED of an optoisolator. The converter output voltage of nominally 155 V is divided down by R2 and R9, a $1/(4.33)$ divider, then translated in voltage through a 35 V zener diode to the input of a NPN BJT used as a comparator. (See 'Control Supply' in 'Battery Charger Circuits' for another example of a BJT comparator.) A BJT is a crude comparator, with a 0.7 V input offset between base and

56

emitter. In this application, however, with 155 V for comparison, it is negligible. The base zener effectively raises the comparison voltage at the divider output to 35.7 V. On the high side of the divider, this becomes (35.7 V)·(4.33) = 155 V. The N1 collector in series with a 9.4 V zener and 18 V supply sets the maximum optoisolator current at under 9 mA.

On the photo-transistor side, emitter voltage is input to a non-inverting op-amp integrator at pin 12. Its feedback is returned to the TL494 5 V reference, thereby setting the noninverting pin operating point at 5 V and the nominal photo-transistor current at 5 V/100 kΩ or 50 µA. When the converter output voltage is too high, N1 conducts more, the photo-BJT emitter voltage rises, it is integrated, and the DTC voltage rises, reducing D and hence the converter drive. The feedback is negative.

To complicate the feedback control loop, two additional inputs to it are shown in the circuit diagram. The first is a DTC input from the undervoltage comparator. *Undervoltage protection* (UVP) is required at power-on and power-off because the voltages of the supplies that drive gates of the power MOSFETs must first be high enough for MOSFETs to be driven on hard (low r_{on}). Inadequate gate drive can cause the MOSFET to operate at a point between full-on and full-off where its channel resistance is high. This leads to excessive power dissipation and MOSFET failure from over-temperature. The UVP circuit output is high during undervoltage. The divider presents its 10.5 V high output to the DTC pin divided to about 3.5 V. DTC is connected through a diode to the feedback integrator so that the op-amp is unable to pull down the voltage at DTC caused by the UVP output. With no undervoltage, the divider resistors both are essentially grounded and present a 1.6 kΩ load to the integrator.

The second injector into the feedback loop is the fan driver circuit. When the fan turns on, the MOSFET driving the fan turns on and grounds its drain. The cathode of the series diode is grounded through it, and through a 10 kΩ resistor discharges the 10 µF capacitor. When it crosses below the op-amp input at 5 V minus a diode drop, the diode connected to pin 12 turns on, reducing the integrator input voltage along with the discharge of the 10 µF capacitor. This reduces the DTC voltage and increases D, causing the converter to drive the output harder.

The fan turns on when a thermistor temperature sensor detects an overtemperature on a primary-circuit MOSFET. Instead of turning off the converter drive because of overtemperature, this circuit increases D instead, causing the converter to drive the output harder. Thus it appears to not have an *overtemperature protection* (OTP) function. It is not uncommon to trace out commercial circuitry only to be puzzled by certain circuits. This one might fall in this category. Its intended function appears to provide thermal feedforward, yet instead of 'throttling back' the converter, it is turned on harder.

Use of the previous equations for currents can clarify the behavior. By extending D, average output current is increased for the same I_s and I_p. MOSFET rms current varies proportional to I_p and $\sqrt{D}$. An increase in D increases $\sqrt{D}$ less than D and the rms current, $\tilde{i}_Q$, is reduced, thereby reducing MOSFET heating. The circuit is indeed a thermal feedforward mechanism intended to cool the MOSFETs somewhat until the fan can do the job. The time constant in the circuit is $(10 \text{ k}\Omega) \cdot (10 \text{ }\mu\text{F}) = 0.1$ s, with a settling time of about 5 times that, or a half second. This is in the range of thermal response time-scales.

Though this circuit appears to work correctly, it also seems to be the cause of what I consider problematic behavior in this inverter in that it interferes with regulation when the fan turns on and off, causing the output voltage to 'glitch'. It can be seen in the brightening and dimming of lighting loads. The idea is right but the implementation is in need of refinement.

Fan Driver

Two 12 V, 3.4 W, 60 mm box fans cool the power devices and are mounted on the rear panel, as shown on the left side in the inverter picture (p. 60). The original fan driver circuit was subject to failure. The fan drive transistor in the original circuit failed in normal operation in all three of my units. The original fan driver is shown below with the modified circuit. D20 and the 10 kΩ resistor go to the voltage control loop, analyzed previously. The LM324 op-amp is used as a comparator to detect overtemperature and overcurrent events.

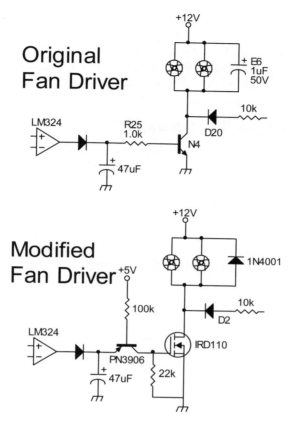

The original circuit used either an NPN BJT or Darlington to drive the two fans. The fan motors are permanent-magnet synchronous types and conduct about 567 mA when running. When the switching transistor turns off, the inductive motor windings conduct this current into the only other path available, the 1 µF capacitor shunting them. The capacitor charges, its voltage increases, and the magnetizing energy of the windings is transferred to the capacitor. When the transistor turns on, it must first conduct away the charge on the capacitor before current will flow through the fan motors. In effect, the 1 µF capacitor is a short to +12V until it discharges. In the modified circuit, the capacitor was replaced with a 1 A diode. The diode conducts the motor current at turn-off while maintaining a diode drop across it. At turn on, the transistor does not conduct a large transient current; diode capacitance is negligible. Also, the BJT was replaced by a small MOSFET capable of conducting 1 A or more.

The input circuit was also modified. The original circuit drove the base through a 1.0 kΩ resistor from a relatively large capacitor. As the capacitor discharges there is a time interval close to turn-off where inadequate base current is provided and the BJT is not fully on, causing it to dissipate excessive power. The modified circuit has instead a PNP that turns off more abruptly when its emitter voltage drops below about 5.7 V, also

Battery Inverter Circuits

turning the MOSFET off abruptly. The modified circuit introduced an additional PNP and resistor, and exchanged an electrolytic capacitor for a diode. The modification fits cleanly into the existing board layout, with a few leads connecting in the air.

Converter designers too often do not know much about motors, and fan drive circuits tend to beg for modification. The above circuit can hopefully provide a template for fan-driver improvement in not only this product but others too.

Op-Amp with Capacitor across Inputs

In the control circuitry of the VEC050D, the battery undervoltage alarm buzzer is driven by another LM324 op-amp. A fragment of this circuit is shown below. The op-amp is configured for use as a comparator with positive feedback, giving the circuit a 10 mV hysteresis, resulting in 10.7 V and 12 V thresholds. The circuit is straightforward except possibly for the large capacitor across the op-amp input terminals. It is intended to keep the buzzer on by causing the input voltage to change slowly between the hysteresis thresholds. This capacitor input scheme is not uncommonly found in low-cost power equipment and other consumer electronics, and is worth a closer look.

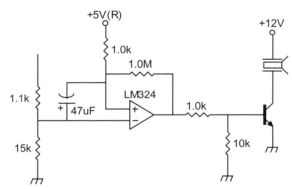

To analyze the circuit, we will do a more general analysis of the effect of placing an impedance, Z_i, across op-amp inputs, by starting with a resistance, R_{in}. Drawing the input error-summing loop of the op-amp more explicitly, as shown below, the error voltage input to the op-amp occurs in an input loop around which are the input voltage, v_i, and the feedback voltage.

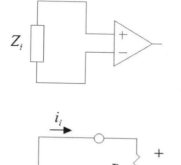

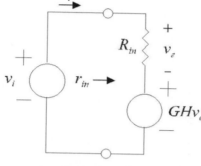

Let the op-amp have an open-loop voltage gain of G and the feedback network a voltage gain (usually attenuation, as a voltage divider) of H. Then the amplifier loop gain is $G \cdot H$. The op-amp input error voltage, v_e, is amplified by the loop gain; v_e is shown across the op-amp input resistance, R_{in}. The $G \cdot H \cdot v_e$ feedback voltage occurs in the loop where it subtracts from v_i;

$$v_e = v_i - G \cdot H \cdot v_e$$

This input-loop equation follows from Kirchhoff's Voltage Law (KVL), and when solved is

$$v_e = \frac{v_i}{1 + G \cdot H}$$

Noting by Ohm's Law (ΩL) that $R_{in} = v_e/i_i$, then dividing each side of the above equation by i_i and substituting,

$$\frac{v_e}{i_i} = R_{in} = \frac{v_i / i_i}{1 + G \cdot H} = \frac{r_{in}}{1 + G \cdot H}$$

61

Battery Inverter Circuits

and the amplifier input resistance,

$$r_{in} = (1 + G \cdot H) \cdot R_{in}$$

The resistance across the op-amp terminals, R_{in}, is effectively larger at the amplifier input by $1 + G \cdot H$. This occurs because the feedback voltage is almost the same as the input voltage, and R_{in} is 'bootstrapped' by the feedback voltage to appear much larger. If instead v_i were across R_{in}, it would be, in effect, only $1/(1 + G \cdot H)$ as large - as is v_e - and i_i would thus be reduced by ΩL by $1 + G \cdot H$. Such is the wonder of feedback.

For the more general case of an impedance, Z_i, across the op-amp input terminals, the analysis still applies, and a capacitor with reactance $Z_i = 1/j\omega \cdot C$ will appear at the input terminals as

$$(1 + G \cdot H)/ j\omega \cdot C$$

or as an equivalent reactance of

$$\frac{1}{j\omega \cdot \left(\dfrac{C}{1 + G \cdot H} \right)}$$

The capacitance is effectively $C/(1 + G \cdot H)$, a capacitance much reduced in value to the external input circuit. Note that the 47 µF used in the alarm circuit is a relatively large value.

Why is this scheme used? It provides common-mode noise filtering at the op-amp input, though it seems like a rather ineffective use of capacitors. If you find an unusual or perplexing circuit - one that might not make much sense, like this one - in a product you trace out, keep in mind that there is always a possibility that it really does *not* make sense! Product designs only need to work sufficiently to sell them. These designs are often able to be refined.

Battery Charger Circuits

Off-line battery chargers appear in the off-grid system as a needed component, to go from a fuel-burning generator or HVDC bus to the battery-bank. In both the 12 V and HVDC system, this is a single component.

Three-State Charging

Three-state lead-acid battery charging begins with a constant current until the battery voltage increases to some nearly-charged value. Then it switches to constant-voltage charging until the battery current decreases to some low value, afterward followed by a slight decrease in voltage to keep the battery 'floating' in the charged state with a *trickle charge*. This charging scheme can also be depicted by the battery voltage and current waveforms shown below.

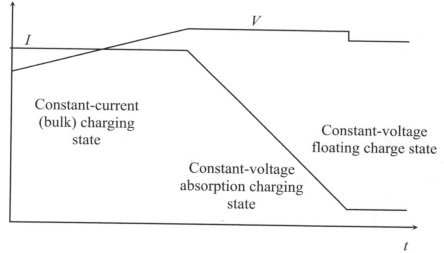

The three-state charging algorithm can also be depicted as a state diagram, shown below, like those used in digital logic design.

Battery Charger Circuits

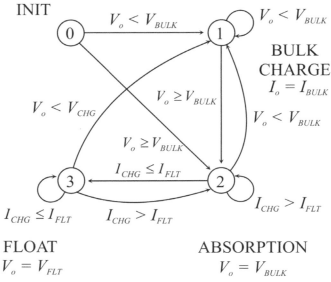

$$INIT$$
$$V_o < V_{BULK}$$
$$V_o < V_{BULK}$$
$$0$$
$$1$$
$$BULK$$
$$CHARGE$$
$$I_o = I_{BULK}$$
$$V_o < V_{CHG}$$
$$V_o \geq V_{BULK}$$
$$V_o < V_{BULK}$$
$$V_o \geq V_{BULK}$$
$$I_{CHG} \leq I_{FLT}$$
$$3$$
$$2$$
$$I_{CHG} > I_{FLT}$$
$$I_{CHG} \leq I_{FLT}$$
$$I_{CHG} > I_{FLT}$$

FLOAT $\qquad\qquad$ ABSORPTION
$$V_o = V_{FLT} \qquad\qquad V_o = V_{BULK}$$

Three-state charging commences with a low battery voltage and constant-current charging at current I_{BULK}. This *bulk-charging* state ends when the battery voltage reaches the preset voltage, V_{BULK}. For a 12 V lead-acid wet cell, this is typically 14.2 V. Then the charger changes to the *absorption* charging state. A constant voltage of V_{BULK} is applied to drive in the harder remaining charge and the charging current is monitored. When it reaches some minimum value indicating that the battery is essentially at full charge, the state is changed to the *floating* state. In this state, a constant voltage, V_{FLT}, is maintained across the battery, but the voltage is lowered from that of the absorption state. Battery charge is maintained by a 'trickle' current and self-discharge is continually 'topped off' at the forced voltage, usually around 13.8 V.

A fourth state can be added, that of *equalization*. This state occurs after the absorption state, when the battery is fully charged. It applies a higher voltage to the battery, around 15 V. This causes a controlled overcharge of most of the battery cells, but weak cells are assured of becoming fully charged so that they do not prematurely fail. The overcharging of stronger cells results in a bubbling away of water which must be replenished after equalization. The equalization state need only be added to the battery charging cycle once every two to four weeks, depending on the age of the batteries, and is not part of the ordinary three-state charging routine.

Schumacher 10 A Charger

Upon tracing the circuitry of a low-cost commercial product, it is possible to be overcome by a desire to redesign some or all of it. I resisted this urge when I repaired two Schumacher 10 A battery chargers. The first charger is a Schumacher 612-A-PE 10 A, 6 V or 12 V charger. Very similar to it but somewhat simplified is a 10 A, 12 V SS-

51A-PE 'Ship 'N Shore' charger. They had identical electronic circuitry, as shown below for the 'Ship 'N Shore' charger.

I requested the technical information from Schumacher. To their credit, I did receive a wiring diagram, but it did not contain the electronics. I consequently had to trace the circuitry of the single-sided board, and my result is given below. (I do not think a competitor would have any trouble tracing the circuitry either, though I doubt that I am the only customer irked by the manufacturer's lack of an 'open source' approach to customer support. Too many of their competitors are no different, however.)

Both products are based on 60 Hz technology, having large 60 Hz transformers with center-tapped secondary windings for full-wave rectification, as shown. Both use rectifier diodes in button packages, mounted with plastic holders onto a metal panel that snaps into the rear half-shell of the case. Four diodes are used, two per side in parallel. These diodes are somewhat obscure Motorola SR4355 Schottky diodes that might better be replaced by a TO-220 or TO-247 three-lead package of common-cathode Schottky diodes, rated around 40 V and 15 A.

The SCR anode is screwed to the metal panel, thereby connecting to the full-wave rectifier output. This pulsating, 120 Hz waveform, v_{in}, will turn off the SCR every cycle. When v_{in} exceeds the battery voltage, V_{BAT}, by a little over a volt, the SCR turns on if its gate is driven. This SCR is not of the 'sensitive gate' type and there is consequently a resistance on the semiconductor chip between gate and cathode of around 300 Ω or less. (This parasitic resistance is the basis for one of the circuit subtleties.) The only IC in the design is the familiar TL431 (designated as R), a three-terminal bandgap reference, op-amp and open-collector output NPN, as shown in the circuit diagram.

Circuit operation is as follows. For $V_{BAT} < 15.0$ V, the voltage divider formed by R10, R12 will place less than 2.5 V on the input (pin 1) of the TL431, causing its output BJT to be off. Then pin 3 is pulled up to V_{BAT} by R7, cutting off Q3 and Q4. With Q3 off, Q2, an inverting BJT, is also off, and Q1 is driven on by R3. It in turn drives on Q7, which drives the SCR gate, turning it on whenever v_{in} is a little above V_{BAT}. R6 limits gate drive current.

When driven on, Q6 turns on somewhat before, and drives Q5 on. It saturates, pulling the input voltage of the TL431 below 2.5 V and forcing the output BJT (at pin 3) off. This insures that Q3 is off and that the gate drive stays on the entire cycle, a half-cycle of the power line. (Turning an SCR off at high current can be rude.)

Battery Charger Circuits

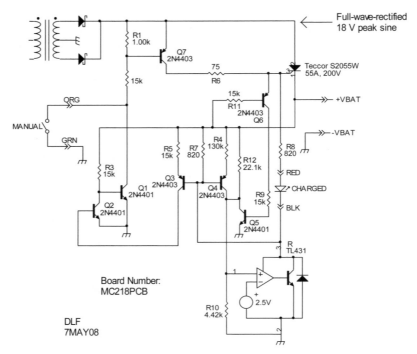

Schumacher SS-51A-PE
10 A, 12 V Battery Charger
Ship 'N Shore

Board Number:
MC218PCB

DLF
7MAY08

When V_{BAT} exceeds 15 V, then during the off part of the cycle, the TL431 input exceeds 2.5 V and its output BJT turns on, pulling pin 3 low. However, it does not saturate, for if it did, it would be hard to explain the function of Q4. When the TL431 output decreases in voltage to about a junction drop below 2.5 V, the collector-base junction of Q4 conducts, connecting the TL431 output to its input. The TL431 loop has negative feedback and will then keep its output around 1.8 V. However, before Q4 saturates, it operates in normal mode and supplies current from R4 to the TL431 input. This positive-feedback hysteresis insures that the TL431 will switch cleanly when the battery voltage is at the borderline voltage. After switching, Q4 then takes on its second function of closing the TL431 loop as a *c-b* diode. This keeps the Q3, Q4 base voltage at 1.8 V and keeps Q3 from saturating as it drives Q2 on and turns off Q1, thereby turning off Q7 gate drive. The charging has ended.

With the TL431 output held at its 1.8 V low state, the CHARGED LED can conduct through the SCR shunt gate-cathode resistance from V_{BAT}. This conduction not only lights the LED, it also applies a small reverse voltage across the SCR gate-cathode input, giving the SCR some margin in remaining off. Without knowing about the SCR shunt resistance, it makes no sense to connect the CHARGED LED circuit to the SCR gate.

The above circuit behavior is for the automatic charger mode, with the MANUAL switch open. What is 'automatic' about it is that charging turns off when the battery voltage reaches 15 V. If the MANUAL switch is on, it forces Q7 and SCR gate drive to be on all the time, requiring the user to watch the battery voltage. This mode, however, also allows the battery to be overcharged, which can be useful for equalizing the cells.

Is this charger design worthy of redesign? It is based on 60 Hz technology, which is larger and weighs and costs more than switching technology. The charging algorithm is simple - too simple. It only charges in voltage-source mode, and unregulated at that. With variations in power-line voltage, the charging current will also vary. With high line voltage, it can be excessive for a while.

It is better to have three-state charging. I overcame the urge to install a current-sense circuit and some additional logic, to implement at least two-state charging. With 60 Hz technology it is not really worth the trouble; better to start with a switching-converter design or buy a switching-converter charger such as those low-cost 25 A or 30 A units sold by Vector Mfg. Co. (Black & Decker). They too break and have more circuitry, but are also repairable, given a circuit diagram. When they work, however (which is most of the time), they work well and are versatile. The 50/60 Hz charger designs are being obsoleted quickly by switchers, a clearly superior solution to the charging problem.

VEC1095 25 A Off-Line Charger

A low-cost, well-designed, and reliable charger (except for the push-buttons!) is the Black & Decker (Vector) VEC1095APB 25 A (or 30 A) charger, capable of charging wet-cell, sealed gel-cell, or sealed AGM 12 V lead-acid batteries. It uses the established three-state charging method. It also uses a switching converter and microcontroller to vastly reduce charger size and weight over the old transformer-based 50 or 60 Hz chargers. Two are shown in operation on the next page.

Line Filter

The 120 V ac input is converted to battery voltage by the circuit shown on page 69. Power switching can generate significant electrical noise or 'electromagnetic interference' (EMI) that requires extensive power-line input filtering to keep from using the power distribution lines as distributors of EMI. The VEC1095 has typical LC filtering, preceded by a board-mount fuse and varistor for overvoltage protection against large power-line transient voltages. C1, L1, C3 form the first LC filter stage, which is all that most line-input converters have. The charger, however, is higher in power than most household electrical appliances. Using Watt's Law, battery charging power is $(12 \text{ V}) \cdot (25 \text{ A}) = 550 \text{ W}$.

Battery Charger Circuits

The second stage of filtering, C2, C3, L2, C8, demonstrates the typical line-input filter of power converters. The two 10 nF capacitors connected to earth or safety ground are the 'Y' capacitors; they form a Y between the two input terminals and ground. They filter out *normal-mode* noise - noise that occurs on one or the other (neutral or line) terminals but not both together, which is *common-mode* noise. It is added to both terminals and is filtered by the 'X' (across) capacitor, C8, following L2.

L1, L2, and L4 are commonly referred to as 'common-mode chokes' and are high-frequency transformers with a turns ratio of one. Any current flowing through one of the windings will induce a voltage across the other winding to drive current in the opposite direction, thus completing the circuit.

Vector Mfg VEC1095APOB 25A Battery Charger

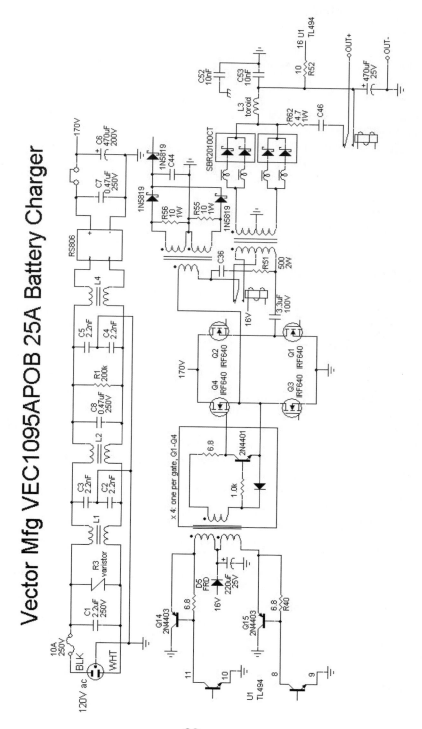

Battery Charger Circuits

In other words, current in either winding will tend to force the same current to flow in the other, to make the currents in both branches of the loop equal. This forces a common-mode current condition so that any current finding a spurious path back to the input will be forced to flow through these transformers instead.

The VEC1095 has three stages of common-mode transformers. They not only attenuate or filter noise from the power-line into the converter, but mainly, converter switching noise is attenuated in the reverse direction of input power flow. Looking back into C8 and L2, C8 provides an easy return path for high-frequency switching noise back to the converter. Similarly, L2 presents a high-impedance path to the power-line for this noise. The first stage of filtering presents a similar scheme.

The Y capacitors C2, C3 are returned to a different connection location at the front of the charger enclosure than are C4, C5, grounded at the rear. Apparently the designers found that spurious capacitive paths for switching currents were better returned from these grounding locations. This illustrates the somewhat elusive character of noise reduction. It can become an experimental activity of searching for what works best.

H-Bridge Gate Driver

The converter is controlled by U1, a TL494 PWM controller IC. Its push-pull outputs drive a center-tapped primary winding of a transformer, with additional current supplied by Q14, Q15. These PNP BJTs shunt additional current to ground that is needed to drive the transformer but would be too much for the TL494 output NPNs to sink. This gate-drive transformer has four secondary windings, one for each MOSFET of the converter full-wave H-bridge. (It is left for the reader to determine where the dots should go on these windings for correct drive phasing.) Q1, Q4 are phased together, being on and off at the same time. Similarly, Q2, Q3 are on together during the opposite half-cycle of transformer current drive. The four IRF640 power MOSFETs are attached to a board-mount heat sink and cooled by forced-air convection from the cooling fan, another of those 12 V dc box fans with sleeve bearings that are often the first items to fail. (See 'Fan Repair' in 'Battery Inverter Circuits'.)

The secondary windings drive the MOSFET gates relative to their sources. Because each winding is isolated from the others, the two high-side windings can 'float' near the 170 V of Q2, Q4 sources when they are on while the Q1, Q3 gate-drive windings remain near ground. The $6.8\ \Omega$ series gate resistance slows the turn-on slightly, to keep excessive voltage spikes from occurring in the H-bridge circuit caused by a fast turn-on change in current. The voltage across any parasitic trace or component lead inductance is $L \cdot di/dt \approx L \cdot \Delta i/t_{sw}$, where t_{sw} is the MOSFET switching time. The diode provides a return path for the gate turn-on current around the transistor.

The NPN BJT of the gate circuit is driven on at turn-off, and it discharges the gate-source capacitance for faster MOSFET turn-off. This is important because H-bridge switches must turn off before the other switch in the half-bridge turns on or else *shoot-through* occurs, whereby both high- and low-side switches are on for a short time, shorting the 170 V supply to ground.

H-Bridge Transformer Flux Balance

The 3.3 µF capacitor in series with the transformer primary winding forces flux balance in the transformer. Transformers driven push-pull must have exactly the same circuit-driven flux each half-cycle to keep from 'ratcheting' up in current without limit. Magnetic flux as 'seen' from the circuit - from the transformer terminals – is

$$\lambda = v \cdot t$$

or the voltage applied to the winding times the time it is applied. This *circuit-referred flux* is also related to inductance and current:

$$\lambda = L \cdot i$$

During a half cycle, a change in flux occurs during the on-time:

$$\Delta\lambda = V_g \cdot \Delta t = V_g \cdot t_{on}$$

A relatively constant supply voltage, V_g, is applied to each half of the primary winding during the on-time of each half-cycle. Not only must the on-times of each half-cycle be equal, the voltage at the transformer terminals must also be equal. Differences in circuit resistance (even winding resistance differences) can upset the perfect balance needed. If the $\Delta\lambda$s do not exactly equal, then

$$\Delta\lambda = L \cdot \Delta i$$

is not the same for both half-cycles, and the Δi of one half-cycle will not cancel the Δi of the other, leaving a Δi difference each half-cycle. This difference accumulates each cycle in the form of a current waveform that ratchets toward a destructive value. This flux imbalance problem is inherent in voltage-driven push-pull converters. It is the same problem that converters in battery inverters can have.

To remedy this problem in the charger, the series capacitor forces flux balance. A difference in Δi results in an accumulating voltage across the 3.3 µF capacitor of a polarity that opposes the difference. The cycle with greater $\Delta\lambda$ will have greater Δi and this will cause the series-C to charge with a voltage that subtracts from the applied winding voltage, V_g, for this half-winding. This reduced voltage reduces the flux. It is a simple, but effective method of flux balance.

Transformers have two currents: the *magnetizing* current which must be controlled by flux balance, and the *secondary-referred* or load current, which is the secondary-

71

Battery Charger Circuits

circuit current as 'seen' in the primary winding (through the turns ratio). The magnetizing current is a triangle waveform while the secondary-referred current waveform follows the load current waveform through transformer behavior.

The series capacitor must be large enough in value to conduct both primary current components without appreciably changing the voltage applied to the primary winding. Additionally, it must be rated to support the primary current. Often, a capacitor of larger capacitive value must be used to provide sufficient conduction area to sustain the required current.

We can estimate the minimum required primary current from an ideal (100 % efficiency) calculation of converter power. The specified nominal output power is 550 W. The converter input voltage is 170 V. The primary current, on average, will then be

$$\frac{550 \text{W}}{170 \text{V}} = 3.24 \text{ A}$$

This is an average, not rms, current but can be used to calculate average power because

$$\bar{p} = V \cdot \bar{i} = \bar{v} \cdot I$$

That is, average power is average current times constant voltage. It is also average voltage times constant current. Average power involving sine waveforms must instead be calculated from rms values of voltage and current.

When the primary winding is switched off, the load current quickly ceases. The magnetizing current flowing in the transformer mutual inductance shared by the windings continues to flow, but through the MOSFET body-drain diodes (p. 30) of the other pair of switches, as shown below.

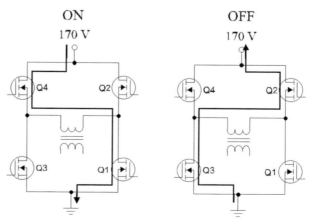

72

Suppose primary current is flowing through Q4 and Q1, and they turn off. The magnetizing part of that current continues to flow in the transformer because of its inductance, and in the same direction as at turn-off. It flows through the body-drain diodes of Q2, Q3: from ground through Q3, the primary winding, Q2 and then into the 170 V supply. The winding current is now flowing against the voltage across its terminals and will decrease at the rate of 170 V/L_p, where L_p is the primary winding inductance. When BJTs (such as power Darlingtons) or IGBTs are used as switches, external diodes must be added across them.

The primary winding has a series RC across it. This is a *snubber* (p. 35). It is used to damp the resonant circuit at turn-off formed by the diode capacitance with circuit parasitic inductance. The capacitor, C36, is large enough to conduct the resonant current yet its reactance must be large at the switching frequency, to avoid shorting the primary winding with R51, a 500 Ω resistor. At the much higher frequency of the switch transition, it is a low reactance and R51 is effectively in parallel with the parasitic parallel resonance, damping it. This resonance is excited by the body-drain diode reverse recovery current and the diode reverse energy is dissipated in R51. We also encounter diode turn-off behavior in the secondary circuit, and its features apply to the snubber resonant circuit.

Current-Sense Circuit

The primary winding is in series with the primary of another transformer with a full-wave, center-tapped rectifier as its secondary circuit. This is a current-sense circuit and the transformer is a 'current transformer'. It is a transformer with a small number of primary turns (often just one) and many secondary turns. The secondary windings are shunted by low-resistance sense resistors, R_s, such as the 10 Ω resistors of this converter. The sense resistors, when referred to the primary winding appear as $n^2 \cdot R_s$. For $n = 1/100$, then for $R_s = 10$ Ω, to the primary it is $R_s' = 1$ mΩ. This low resistance is desirable because a current sense circuit should not introduce additional resistance into the loop of the sensed current. The scale factor of secondary voltage to primary current, or $V_s/I_p = (n \cdot I_p) \cdot R_s$ is 0.1 Ω (100 mV/A) for the given n.

Schottky diodes are used as rectifiers because of the switching frequency of the waveform from the H-bridge. Schottky and fast-recovery diodes (FRDs) are used extensively in switched-power circuits because they can switch quickly. Schottky diodes are limited to lower voltages (typically under 100 V) and have less on-voltage than FRDs, making them more efficient for low-voltage circuits. C44 holds the average voltage. An additional Schottky diode is placed in series with the two rectifier diodes to subtract their voltage drop in compensation, to recover the sensed voltage across the two R_s.

Secondary Circuit

The VEC1095 converter secondary winding is center-tapped with diodes on each end - a full-wave rectifier. The Schottky diodes are packaged in pairs, with a common

Battery Charger Circuits

cathode, as shown. They are used in parallel to double current capability. Inductive beads are placed on the diode leads to modify diode turn-off currents. Diode turn-off at high speed is troublesome. The waveforms are shown below.

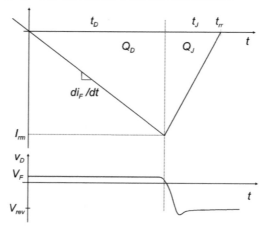

The diode begins forward-biased, with its conducting voltage of V_F across it. Then current is decreased at a high rate, di_F/dt. Current passes through zero. Ideally, the diode is now off. However, when semiconductor junctions have been conducting, higher concentrations of charge exist in the n and p materials. This *diffusion charge*, Q_D, must be removed before the junction is off. The area of the current waveform is the charge. ($q = i \cdot t$) A current flows in the opposite direction until this charge is removed, and it can reach a high peak value, I_{rm}, before the diode voltage collapses to zero volts. Then the reverse voltage across the diode, V_{REV}, becomes quickly established, and as it does the now-off junction behaves as a capacitor and additional junction charge is removed to charge it to the reverse voltage ($V_{REV} = Q_J/C_J$). The area of this charge is shown as Q_J, and flows as the reverse 'recovery' current decreases to zero.

The total time taken for both Q_D and Q_J to be moved through the junction is the diode *reverse recovery time*, t_{rr}. Typically, $t_D > t_J$ and diode manufacturers try to minimize it, to minimize I_{rm}. For the designer using diodes, the consequences of a current spike of I_{rm} must be reduced through reduction of di_F/dt, if possible. The current slope can be decreased by placing in series with the diode a small inductance - the bead inductors in the given circuit. Then according to the v-i relationship for inductances,

$$\frac{di_F}{dt} = \frac{v_L}{L}$$

A large di_F/dt causes a significant voltage drop across the bead inductor of a polarity that opposes current change, thus contributing to a decrease in di_F/dt in the circuit. Put simply, just as the voltage across a capacitor does not change instantaneously, the

74

current through an inductor does not either. The beads will tend to sustain the value of current, causing the depleting junction to do so more slowly as di_F/dt is decreased. While it is desired that t_{rr} be minimized, it is better to increase it if I_{rm} can be decreased.

Another technique for alleviating diode turn-off is that used in the primary circuit, of placing a series RC across the diode(s), thus providing a low-impedance path for the reverse diode current. Such diodes are in series with inductor L3. For each half of the transformer flux cycle, a secondary winding half conducts and they alternate in on-time and off-time conduction. The 470 μF output capacitor filters the ripple of the inductor current for a constant output voltage. The battery load is effectively a huge capacitance (of several farads), though it is at the other end of the charger cables. To stabilize the voltage and the control loop inside the charger, the output capacitor is added.

Buck Converter Circuit

Converter analysis thus far has been about circuit details. We now step back to ask what kind of converter this is. It is a *buck* (*common-passive*) converter, used when $V_g > V_o$. In this case, $V_g = 170$ V and $V_o = 12$ V. However, it also has a transformer and a full-bridge primary circuit. This converter combination is often called a *forward* converter: a transformer-coupled buck converter.

The buck converter can be explained more easily by starting with its simplest form in the figure below. A common feature of basic switching converters is the single-pole, double throw switch, S, in series with the inductor, L. For a buck converter, the switch is at the input and the D' or passive position is connected to the common (ground) terminal shared by input and output. In the charger, the H-bridge, transformer, and secondary diodes function as the switch, with the additional effect of the transformer turns ratio. A simpler one-transistor, one-diode implementation is shown on the right. The MOSFET transistor is the active on-time switch, and the diode is the passive off-time switch that conducts when the MOSFET is off.

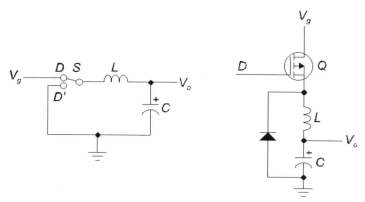

When switch S is on, current from V_g increases through L, charging C and supplying current to the load connected across V_o. The inductor current reaches a maximum when S switches off. The current in an inductor cannot change instantaneously and when S

75

Battery Charger Circuits

switches off, the inductor current will then flow from ground, through the diode and into the inductor. The current is now opposed by the voltage across L, which is now positive at the V_o terminal. The current decreases and C will discharge when the load current exceeds the inductor current. The charging and discharging of C causes voltage variation, an 'ac' or *ripple* voltage component at the output. At the end of the switching cycle, S switches on and the sequence repeats.

S is switched between position D (at V_g) to D' (ground) by control circuits (not shown). The fraction of the switching period that the switch is in position D (or on) is the *duty ratio* (or duty cycle),

$$D = \frac{t_{on}}{t_{on} + t_{off}} = \frac{t_{on}}{T_s} = 1 - D'$$

where t_{on} and t_{off} are the *on-* and *off-times* of S. The total (on + off) time is the switching period, T_s. The output voltage is controlled by controlling D. The TL494 has a switching frequency of about 330 kHz per half cycle, or about 165 kHz for a full cycle. Then $T_s = 1/f_s = 3.06$ µs.

When S is on, the input voltage is applied to the input side of the inductor, L. Under normal operation, the capacitor is charged to the desired output voltage, V_o. The voltage across L is then $V_g - V_o$. The rate of change (or slope) of the current in the inductor is

$$\frac{v_L}{L} \cong \frac{\Delta i_L}{\Delta t}$$

where the change in inductor current, Δi_L, and Δt are small. During the on-time,

$$\frac{V_g - V_o}{L} \cong \frac{\Delta i_L}{\Delta t} = \frac{\Delta i_L}{t_{on}}$$

With S on, i_L increases (because $\Delta i_L / \Delta t > 0$), as shown below.

76

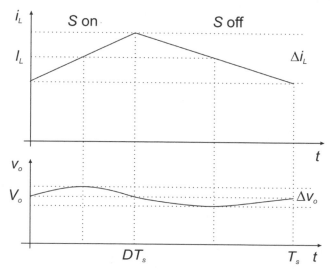

S turns off at time $D \cdot T_s$, when inductor and switch current is maximal. This peak current value is a factor in the current rating for both the MOSFET and diode. The converter voltage gain or voltage transfer function, V_o / V_g, is controlled by D and can be derived by equating Δi_L of the on- and off-times. If a constant average current in the inductor is maintained (that is, steady-state operation), then over the switching cycle, Δi_L must equal zero if the average current is to stay the same. Solving

$$\frac{v_L}{L} \cong \frac{\Delta i_L}{\Delta t}$$

for Δi_L and applying it to the on-time, the change in current is

$$\Delta i_L (\text{on}) = \frac{(V_g - V_o) \cdot (D \cdot T_s)}{L}$$

The off-time is the remainder of the switching period after the on-time, or

$$t_{off} = T_s - D \cdot T_s = (1 - D) \cdot T_s = D' \cdot T_s$$

During the off-time, the inductor current change is

$$\Delta i_L (\text{off}) = -\frac{(-V_o) \cdot ((1 - D) \cdot T_s)}{L}$$

77

Battery Charger Circuits

Then for a stable average of I_L, $\Delta i_L(\text{on}) = -\Delta i_L(\text{off})$, and

$$\frac{(V_g - V_o) \cdot (D \cdot T_s)}{L} = \frac{V_o \cdot ((1-D) \cdot T_s)}{L}$$

Solving for the transfer function, it is simply

$$\frac{V_o}{V_g} = D$$

The output voltage is proportional to D and V_g.

The simple buck circuit analysis applies to the charger converter, though the transformer turns ratio must be taken into account. Then the transfer functions for both voltage and current are

$$\frac{V_o}{V_g} = \frac{I_g}{I_o} = \frac{1}{n} \cdot D, n = \frac{N_p}{N_s}$$

where N is number of winding turns. With the additional parameter n, for nominal V_g and V_o, D is free to be set at an optimal value.

The transformer secondary voltages and currents for on- and off-times are shown below, simplified to one diode per side.

On-time currents

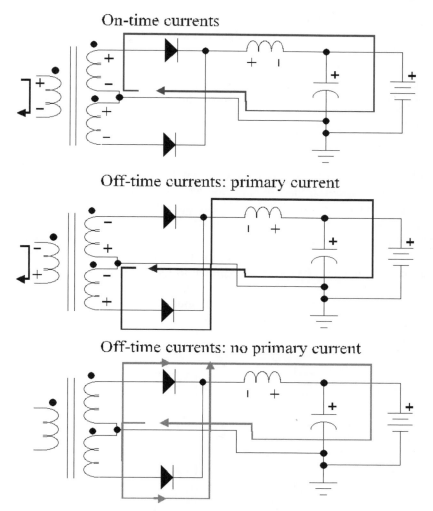

Off-time currents: primary current

Off-time currents: no primary current

The on-time switches in the charger are the H-bridge switch-pairs of each half-cycle and one of the two pairs of secondary diodes. What is shown during the on-time is the half-cycle during which the dotted ends of the windings are driven positive. The secondary winding sources current through the upper diode to the load and back through ground.

At off-time, the primary current decreases, causing the winding voltage polarities to reverse, as shown in the middle circuit. Then the other diode conducts the output inductor current. The third (lowest drawing) circuit state assumes that the magnetizing current in the primary decreases to zero and ceases - the discontinuous-current mode (DCM). In this case, the winding voltages collapse, yet inductor current continues to flow, split about equally through both secondary windings.

Ordinarily the converter would operate in continuous-current mode (CCM) and the third state of off-time DCM would not occur. Consequently, the two diode branches

79

Battery Charger Circuits

alternate in conduction, each conducting the entire cycle though alternating their on- and off-times. This causes the diodes to conduct the same average and rms currents over a range of duty-ratio.

A relay switches the primary turns through a tap on the primary winding, changing n. This allows the converter to run at an optimum D when changing output voltage, such as during the equalization state. For a forward converter, the optimal D is near the high end of the range, for then $\kappa_Q = \kappa_D = 1/\sqrt{D}$ are minimized. (For more on κ, see p. 18.)

Control Supply

The VEC1095 control supply is also a switching converter. It is an isolated common-inductor configuration or *flyback* converter that uses a *transductor* (transformer or coupled inductor) as a coupled inductor. The circuit diagram, as I traced it, is shown below. The circuit works basically as follows. Q5 is the active power switch, a common TIP50 BJT. When it turns on, about 170 V is applied to the primary winding of the transductor. The current ramps up and the voltage across sense resistor, R5, increases until it reaches the threshold base-emitter voltage of Q6 - about 0.5 V - when it begins to conduct in earnest. Q6 collector current diverts current through R15 from the base of Q5 until Q5 is unable (because of its finite β) to conduct the winding current. It begins to divert to the primary voltage clamp through D3.

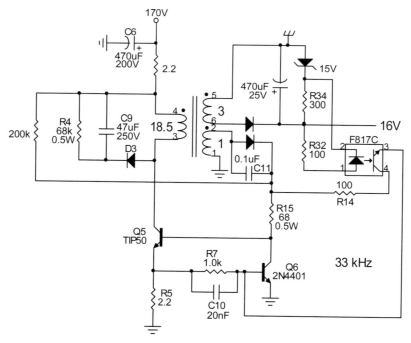

During this on-time, the lower secondary winding has been supplying the base current of Q5 through a diode. By the winding dot convention, the dotted positive terminal of the primary winding causes the dotted side of the secondary feedback winding to also be positive with respect to primary-side ground. When Q5 begins to shut off and current decreases, the winding voltages reverse in polarity. This causes the feedback winding to reinforce the turn-off of Q5. The output secondary winding begins to conduct and the nominal 16 V output begins to increase somewhat.

Turn-on occurs when the secondary current decreases to zero. The transductor flux collapses and the feedback winding voltage increases from its negative value to zero, causing a positive voltage to be applied through C11 to provide base current to Q5, turning it on. C11 was charged during the off-time through the 200 kΩ resistor to the 170 V input supply. After Q5 turns on, continuing positive drive through the feedback winding keeps it on. The nifty feature of this simple control scheme is that it starts the next cycle immediately after secondary current is zero, thereby keeping the converter operating at the boundary between CCM and DCM.

Regulation of the output voltage is accomplished by a crude kind of comparator circuit. R34 supplies current through a 15 V zener diode, which provides a voltage reference at the cathode of an optoisolator LED. As the output voltage increases, current through the LED is determined by R32. The optoisolator has a current gain that can vary from 0.2 to 1 among different units. During the on-time, current is supplied from the feedback winding voltage through R14 and the phototransistor to the base of Q6, where it develops a voltage across R7 and R5. This voltage adds to the sense voltage developed by the Q5 emitter current through R5 and thereby varies the peak primary current at which Q6 will begin to conduct, thus ending the on-time. This voltage threshold is simply the v-i curve of the b-e diode junction of Q6 and it varies with temperature. As the circuit heats, the threshold voltage decreases, offering some protection as a side-effect.

The tight feedback loop formed by Q5, Q6 has an incremental (small-signal) current gain that can be approximated as follows. First, Q6 base voltage is

$$v_{be6} = r_{in} \cdot i_i \approx \{R_7 \,||\, (\beta_6 + 1) \cdot r_{e6}\} \cdot i_i$$

where r_e is incremental emitter resistance of about 26 mV/$|I_E|$. Then Q6 base voltage results in a collector current of

$$i_{c6} = \alpha_6 \cdot \frac{v_{be6}}{r_{e6}} = \beta_6 \cdot \left(\frac{R_7}{R_7 + (\beta_6 + 1) \cdot r_{e6}} \right) \cdot i_i$$

Continuing around the loop,

$$v_{c6} = v_{b5} \approx i_{c6} \cdot [R_{15} \,||\, (\beta_5 + 1) \cdot (r_{e5} + R_5)]$$

for $R_7 \gg R_5$. From the v_{b5} node back to the input, the gain is

$$\frac{v_{be6}}{v_{b5}} \approx \frac{R_5}{R_5 + r_{e5}} \cdot \frac{(\beta_6 + 1) \cdot r_{e6}}{(\beta_6 + 1) \cdot r_{e6} + R_7}$$

The output current is i_{c5}. Altogether, the closed-loop current gain expression, when simplified, is

$$\frac{i_{c5}}{i_i} = \frac{i_p}{i_{opto}} \approx \left(\frac{R_{15}}{R_{15}/\beta_5 + r_{e5}}\right) \cdot \left(\frac{R_7}{R_7/\beta_6 + r_{e6}}\right)$$

$$\approx \left(\frac{68\,\Omega}{68\,\Omega/5}\right) \cdot \left(\frac{1\,k\Omega}{1\,k\Omega/200 + 115\,\Omega}\right) \approx 42$$

Q5 conducts tens of mA and its r_e is negligible. Q5, when on, should be in saturation and its β will not be high; $\beta_5 = 10$ is assumed here. In deep saturation, it would not even be that high. Then if the peak primary current is

$$(0.5\ \text{V})/\text{R5} = (0.5\ \text{V})/(2.2\ \Omega) = 227\text{mA}$$

peak Q5 base current (at turn-off) is about 22.7 mA. A percent of this is beginning to be a significant amount, or 227 µA. For it, r_{e6} is about 115 Ω and the Q5, Q6 loop current gain is the calculated value of 42. Variation in β among BJTs is wide and this loop gain also varies widely depending on both BJT parameters β and r_e.

The change in duty-ratio, D, with output voltage can be approximated by noting that the change in optoisolator current required to change V_{BE}(Q6) by 0.1 V is $(0.1\ \text{V})/(R_7 + R_5) \approx 100$ µA. With the minimum optoisolator current gain (called 'CTR' in manufacturer part data) of 0.2, corresponding to an opto-LED current change of 0.5 mA, then the change in output voltage occurs across the opto-LED in series with $R_{32} = 100$ Ω. The opto incremental resistance will be 26 mV/$|I_{LED}|$. If I_{LED} is 1 mA or more, then LED incremental resistance < 26 Ω. A change in 100 µA develops from a change in output voltage across roughly a range of $R_{32} + 25$ Ω to $R_{32} + 75$ Ω or 125 Ω to 200 Ω, corresponding to about 10 mV to 20 mV. Given the Q6 threshold voltage of 0.5 V, then 0.1 V of change from 10 to 20 mV of output change varies the on-time by about 0.1 V/0.5 V or 20 %. If D is around 0.5, then it varies D by about 10 %.

The flyback power-converter stage has a transfer function of

$$\frac{V_o}{V_g} = \frac{1}{n} \cdot \frac{D}{1-D} = \frac{1}{n} \cdot \frac{D}{D'}$$

where n is the primary/secondary turns ratio, which in this case is $18.5/3 \approx 6.2$. The nominal D for this converter can be solved for and is found to be $D_{nom} = 0.58$; optimal D for flyback converters is typically 0.5, and this is somewhat close. Then the incremental change in output voltage, v_o, with incremental change in D, or d, is

$$\frac{v_o}{d} = \frac{V_g}{n} \cdot \left(\frac{1}{D'} + \frac{D}{D'^2} \right) = \frac{V_g}{n} \cdot \left(\frac{1}{D'^2} \right)$$

Then for $D_{nom} = 0.58$,

$$v_o/d = [(170 \text{ V})/6.2] \cdot [1/(1 - 0.58)]^2 = 27.4 \cdot 5.67 = 155 \text{ V}$$

which is equal to the large-signal gain, V_o/D. The incremental feedback gain, d/v_o can be improved given D_{nom}. With Q6 off, the $v_{be}(Q6)/v_o$ gain is about

$$\frac{v_{be}(Q6)}{v_o} \approx \frac{R7}{R32 + r_{LED}} \cdot A_I(\text{opto}) \approx \frac{1\,\text{k}\Omega}{200\,\Omega} \cdot 0.2 = 1$$

using minimum opto-isolator gain. The variation of a current ramp in on-time with $v_{be}(Q6)$ is $dt_{on}/v_{be}(Q6) = t_{on}/V_{BE}(\text{thr}) = D \cdot T_s/0.5$ V, where dt_{on} is an incremental Δt_{on} (not d times t_{on}). The measured flyback converter switching frequency is $f_s = 1/T_s = 155$ kHz. Then $T_s = 6.45$ μs, nominal on-time is 3.74 μs and $dt_{on}/v_{be}(Q6) = 7.48$ μs/V. On-time varies with D as $dt_{on}/d = T_s = 1/f_s$. Then

$$\frac{d}{v_{be}(Q6)} = \frac{dt_{on}/v_{be}(Q6)}{dt_{on}/d}$$

$$= \frac{dt_{on}/v_{be}(Q6)}{T_s} = \frac{7.48\,\mu s/V}{6.45\,\mu s} = 1.16\,\text{V}^{-1} = 1/0.86\,\text{V}$$

Thus a 10 % change in D corresponds to a change in v_{BE} of 86 mV.

The complete feedback-path transfer function results from these derivations as

Battery Charger Circuits

$$\frac{d}{v_o} = \frac{d}{v_{be}(Q6)} \cdot \frac{v_{be}(Q6)}{v_o} \approx 1.16 \text{ V}^{-1} = 1/0.86 \text{ V}$$

A change in D of 1 (full range) corresponds to a change in V_O of 0.86 V. The loop gain is the converter (forward-path) gain multiplied by the feedback-path gain, or

$$\frac{v_o}{d} \cdot \frac{d}{v_o} = \frac{155 \text{ V}}{0.86 \text{ V}} = 180$$

This gain is not huge but is quite sufficient for many power supplies not requiring highly accurate output voltages.

This power supply appears to be adequate for non-precision applications, which are many. Linear post-regulators can be used to achieve higher output performance at lower efficiency. With its minimal parts count and no PWM controller IC cost, why are these kinds of minimalist supplies not used more widely? One reason is that they violate the dictum of stable circuit design that requires circuit performance to be relatively independent of BJT parameters. In this case, two comparators are implemented minimally. The first is the output voltage comparator implemented with the optoisolator LED. The optoisolator becomes a differential current-input amplifier, or transresistance amplifier, with an input offset voltage equal to the LED diode on-voltage. This is hardly precision amplification! Yet for margins of a small number of tens of mV, it is quite satisfactory. The LED on-voltage does not change much with LED error current, which does not change much with a small error in V_O.

The other simple comparator is the off-time comparator. Again, it is a p-n junction, the b-e junction of Q6. Q6 is hardly a precision comparator. It is a one-BJT transconductance amplifier with an input offset voltage of V_{BE} with -2.2 mV/°C temperature drift, and has an input bias current of microamperes. The feedback loop that it forms with Q5 does not aid the comparator switching behavior either, for as Q6 current increases, causing Q5 to be turning off, its emitter voltage decreases, driving Q6 toward turn-off instead of increased turn-on. The off-time switching is dependent on the feedback winding drive. At the collector of Q5, the turn-off transition has a pronounced hesitation before the voltage decreases rapidly in better switching behavior. This reduces converter efficiency.

The dynamic response of this circuit is limited by the flyback, or D/D', circuit type (*topology*), which delays delivery of power to the output until the off-time of the cycle. This however does not fault the minimalist implementation, which has the dynamics advantage of being peak-current controlled. Peak-current detection is compensated by C10, to form a compensated voltage divider to v_{be}, compensating for C_{be} of Q6. The 20 μs time constant of R7, C10 is slower that the Q6 current-bandwidth time constant, τ_β ($\tau_\beta = \beta/(2 \cdot \pi \cdot f_T)$), and thus behaves as a phase-lead compensator, reducing the delay in turn-off of Q5 and the start of off-time. This can be important at power-on, with $V_O = 0$ V, for then off-time current in the secondary decays slowly and D can be very small. At low V_O, C11 will not pulse the base of Q5 much either, leading to a weak turn-on. This is compensated in part by the reduced current through the opto-BJT which increasingly biases Q6 off. Only two stages in the transistor part of the loop reduce its loop delay and transient response time.

The switching scheme for this implementation is not as high in loop gain and therefore switching time is not as short as for more elaborate converter controllers. This causes higher switching loss. Use of a power BJT for Q5 also leads to lower efficiency because of base drive; R15 is a half-watt resistor. However, slower switching times also reduce EMI and spurious spiking.

Designers should not necessarily abandon integrated op-amps or comparators, though it is good to keep these simpler, lower-performance options in mind. Design optimization involves tradeoffs between conflicting criteria, and where a cheaper, lower-parts-count circuit can provide the needed function with adequate performance, it might well be optimal. If you are not involved in design, you still can assess the quality of the circuits in a power-system product. Products designed to be manufactured in low labor-rate places tend to use more low-cost parts leading to a different style of design than those from high-performance, higher-cost sources. Such circuit assessment skills can be useful in evaluating circuits in products and in making repeat-purchase product selection decisions.

Wind Converter Circuits

Wind generators can be designed and built from commonly-available blade kits and motors, used as generators. Tails and speed-limiting mechanisms are additional mechanical components, all placed at the top of a pole which can be hinged at the bottom and held up by carbuncle-tensioned guy wires anchored in concrete footers. The generator can be brought down with a winch for maintenance by releasing the carbuncles.

Wind generators are often a complementary source of electric power when the sun is not available. Small commercial wind generators usually supply electronics for 12 or 24 V battery charging. Solar chargers are usually designed to also interface to wind generators for which their main function is to control load dumping of excess power. Wind generators are kept loaded to keep them from spinning too fast, though if the additional power is not needed, it must be dissipated in a giant resistor bank. What is better is to store and recover this excess power, if possible.

Electrical-Mechanical Conversion

The two mechanical quantities of interest are rotational force, or torque, T, and rotational speed, ω_{me}. Because this speed is rotational, it is also referred to as the *mechanical frequency*. Torque is measured in ounce-inches, foot-pounds, or newton-meters. It is related to the tangential force at right angle to a radius vector of length r by

$$T = r \cdot F_{\perp}$$

There are 141.6 oz·in per N·m. Rotational speed is measured in either revolutions (or cycles) per minute (rev/min or rpm), or cycles per second, in the unit of hertz (Hz), or in radians per seconds (s^{-1}). There are $2 \cdot \pi$ radians of angle per cycle.

Mechanical power is

$$P_{me} = T \cdot \omega_{me}$$

Electrical power is expressed by Watt's Law;

$$P_{el} = v \cdot i$$

where v is voltage, in units of volts (V) and i is current, in ampères (A). In electromechanical power conversion, the electrical and mechanical power are equal, assuming no loss due to conversion inefficiencies;

$$P_{me} = P_{el}$$

Generator Parameters and Conversion Relationships

The generator has two parameters of importance to converter design: electromechanical flux, λ_{me}, and winding resistance, R. These parameters are chosen based on torque and speed range specifications. The conversion parameter λ_{me} is often referred to in motor manufacturer data as the 'voltage constant', K_V or K_E, or 'torque constant', K_T. They are usually given in units such as V/krpm or N·m/A. These units are equivalent to within a scale factor;

$$\frac{\text{N} \cdot \text{m}}{\text{A}} \equiv \text{V} \cdot \text{s} = \frac{\text{V}}{\text{s}^{-1}}$$

They are essentially the same parameter. A volt-second is a unit of magnetic flux. The symbol, λ_{me}, is that of the circuit-referred flux amplitude of the generator from the mechanical frame of reference. The magnetic field flux, ϕ, is related to the circuit flux by the turns, N, as

$$\lambda = N \cdot \phi$$

The mechanical reference-frame is that of the generator shaft which turns at the speed of ω_{me}. The circuit-referred speed is the frequency of the winding voltage and is the number of motor pole-pairs times ω_{me}. Thus λ_{me} is the circuit flux relative to the mechanical speed and torque. This electrical-mechanical conversion parameter appears in two basic equations relating the mechanical and electrical 'sides' of the generator. The first relates generator speed to its winding voltage;

$$v_{\omega} = \lambda_{me} \cdot \omega_{me}$$

where v_{ω} is the open-circuit voltage at the motor terminals, induced by the rotor moving past the stator windings. This 'speed voltage' varies with the motor mechanical speed and is the generator output voltage.

The second basic electromechanical relationship is between torque and current;

$$T = \lambda_{me} \cdot i_s$$

where i_s is the stator current, the terminal current of the generator.

Mechanical and electrical systems can both be represented as networks of interconnected components. They are *analogous* in that they show the same behaviors between corresponding quantities and elements. There are two possible correspondences. One of them relates torque (or force) to voltage; the other relates torque to current. Both voltage and speed are 'across' quantities in that they are measured with respect to some other reference point. For voltage, the 0 V reference is *ground*. For speed, it is whatever is considered stationary. Torque (or force) and current are 'through' quantities. Therefore, it is most intuitive to relate like quantities, and the torque-current analogy is preferred and used here.

Once either of these analogies is chosen, then the correspondences of all other electrical and mechanical quantities and elements are determined. For the torque-current analogy, they are listed below.

Mechanical	Electrical
torque, T	current, i
rotational speed, ω_{me}	voltage, v
rotational inertia, J	capacitance, C
compliance, K	inductance, L
1/torsional damping, $1/D_\theta$	resistance, R

Electric machines (motors-generators) are both electrical and mechanical. To model them, it is possible to use a mechanical-electrical analogy and express either the electrical or mechanical 'side' of the generator as the other, so that analysis or design can be carried out on what is either an electrical circuit or a mechanical 'circuit'. In the approach taken here, because the intent is electrical design, the mechanical side of the generator and its attached mechanical source is converted to electrical equivalents. How this is done will be presented after considering the basic characteristics of electric machines, both when motoring and generating. Though our interest is in *generators*, the approach taken here is to use motors as generators. Consequently, some familiarity with electric machines as motors is desirable.

Motor Behavior

A motor to be used as a generator has a torque-speed curve as shown below when motoring.

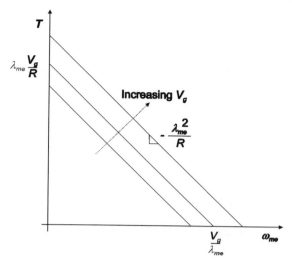

V_g is the voltage applied by a voltage source to the motor terminals. The maximum speed occurs at zero torque:

$$\omega_0 = \frac{V_g}{\lambda_{me}} = \text{no-load mechanical speed}$$

and the maximum torque occurs at zero speed;

$$T_0 = \lambda_{me} \cdot I_0 = \lambda_{me} \cdot \left(\frac{V_g}{R}\right) = \text{stall torque}$$

The stall current, corresponding to T_0, is

$$I_0 = \frac{V_g}{R}$$

The torque-speed function can be derived from the conversion relationships and the basic electric machine model, shown below.

Wind Converter Circuits

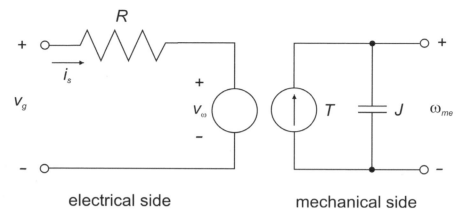

electrical side   mechanical side

In this model, the mechanical side of the generator is represented by its electrical analog. Torque output is from a current source. The rotational inertia, J, is the rotor inertia. On the electrical side, the induced voltage source, v_ω, is in series with winding resistance, R.

The torque-speed function of the motor is derived beginning with the terminal-voltage equation for the electrical side with stator current, i_s;

$$V_g = i_s \cdot R + v_\omega$$

Solve for i_s and substitute it into the torque conversion relationship:

$$T = \lambda_{me} \cdot i_s = \lambda_{me} \cdot \left(\frac{V_g - v_\omega}{R} \right)$$

Then substitute into v_ω from the conversion relationship for the induced voltage. The motor torque-speed equation results:

$$T(\omega_{me}) = -\frac{\lambda_{me}^2}{R} \cdot \omega_{me} + \lambda_{me} \cdot \frac{V_g}{R} = T_0 \cdot \left(1 - \frac{\omega_{me}}{\omega_0} \right)$$

The maximum power, P_{max}, occurs for $T(\omega_{me})$ at $(\omega_0/2, T_0/2)$, where

$$P_{max} = \frac{V_g \cdot I_0}{4}$$

90

Generator Behavior

The terminal voltage, V_g, sources current into the motor terminals, causing it to flow into the induced-voltage source positive terminal. This is the opposite direction to what the v_ω source would cause current to flow. Consequently, it sinks rather than sources power, and this power is converted to mechanical power. It reappears as torque across a positive speed.

For motoring, current supplied by an external current source is sunk by the voltage source on the electrical side, as shown below (top circuit). For the generator, on the mechanical side, the torque current source sinks mechanical power as a reversed speed (voltage) source causes torque, T, to flow through a reversed, negative ω_{me} speed source, as shown (bottom circuit).

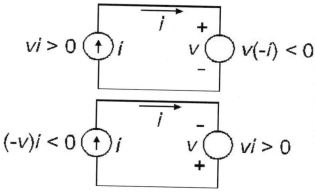

Both the voltage source, v_ω, when motoring and current source, T, when generating have negative power; that is, they sink power instead of source it. For the motor, the external power source is electrical, with positive source power.

For the generator, the external speed source (the propeller) causes the shaft to turn in a direction opposite to what T would cause, and the current source, T, sinks power from the speed source, which is analogously a voltage source supplying $-\omega_{me}$ across T. The torque current source therefore *sinks* power which is converted and sourced as an inverted v_ω on the electrical side where i_s flows in the same direction as shown in the model (into the + electrical terminal). However, it now flows into the negative side of the v_ω source, which sources power to the electrical terminals. The voltage appearing across the terminals, due to the polarity reversal of v_ω, is opposite that shown in the above model. By reversing the generator leads, the correct polarity can be applied to the converter input, and will henceforth be assumed positive.

The generator torque opposing the propeller is

$$T = \lambda_{me} \cdot i_s$$

Wind Converter Circuits

Then for an equivalent load resistance of R_g presented across the electrical terminals by the wind converter input,

$$i_s = \frac{v_\omega}{R + R_g}$$

where the generator induced voltage,

$$v_\omega = \lambda_{me} \cdot \omega_{me}$$

Then combining these in the torque equation,

$$T(\omega_{me}) = \lambda_{me} \cdot i_s = \lambda_{me} \cdot \frac{\lambda_{me} \cdot \omega_{me}}{R + R_g} = \frac{\lambda_{me}^2}{R + R_g} \cdot \omega_{me}$$

Unlike that of the motor, the generator $T(\omega_{me})$ line begins at the T-ω_{me} origin and with positive slope increases with ω_{me}, as shown below.

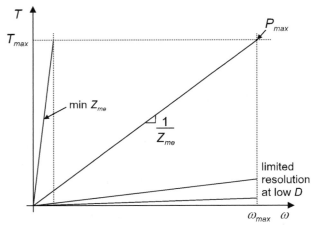

Electromechanical Impedance Transformation

The above torque equation has embedded within it a mechanical resistance or impedance, Z_{me}, analogous to electrical resistance. The impedance relationship between the electrical and mechanical sides can be derived from the basic conversion relations. The electrical impedance of the generator, as measured across its terminals, is

$$Z_g = \frac{v_g}{i_s} = \frac{i_s \cdot R + \lambda_{me} \cdot \omega_{me}}{i_s} = R + \frac{\lambda_{me} \cdot \omega_{me}}{T / \lambda_{me}}$$

$$= R + \lambda_{me}^2 \cdot \frac{\omega_{me}}{T} = R + \lambda_{me}^2 \cdot Z_{me} = R + Z_{me}'$$

where

$$Z_{me} = \frac{\omega_{me}}{T}, \ Z_{me}' = \lambda_{me}^2 \cdot Z_{me}$$

By choosing the speed-voltage analogy, Z_{me} is intuitively the analogous voltage (or speed) divided by the analogous current (or torque) and an analogous mechanical Ohm's Law emerges. The conversion factor (analogous to the turns ratio of a transformer) is λ_{me}. For impedance transformation, as in a transformer, it is λ_{me}^2. Any mechanical load expressed using the speed-voltage analogy can be referred to the electrical side of the generator by λ_{me}^2, and any electrical impedance can similarly be referred to the mechanical side as

$$Z_{el}' = \frac{R + R_g}{\lambda_{me}^2}$$

where R_g is the external impedance across the generator terminals. The generator torque equation can therefore be written in the following electromechanical form of Ohm's Law:

$$T(\omega_{me}) = \frac{\omega_{me}}{(R + R_g) / \lambda_{me}^2} = \frac{\omega_{me}}{Z_{el}'}$$

where the denominator is the total resistance on the electrical side *referred* to the mechanical side as Z_{el}' by the conversion factor λ_{me}^2.

To gain an intuitive understanding of mechanical impedance, consider a current source driving the electrical side as a motor. A current source appears as an open circuit and $Z_{el}' \rightarrow \infty$ as will Z_{el}. A high mechanical impedance requires little torque to produce high speed (just as a high electrical resistance requires little current to develop significant voltage), and the shaft spins easily. But for a voltage-source drive, $Z_{el}' = R/\lambda_{me}^2$, and for small winding R (which is usually the case), the shaft will be stiff. Because a voltage source has zero impedance, a voltage source drive effectively shorts

Wind Converter Circuits

the motor terminals so that any mechanical rotation of the shaft will cause significant current to flow on the electrical side, producing significant counter-torque.

Generator current is controlled by varying R_g. This varies Z_{el}', as shown on the previous graph as 1/slope of $T(\omega_{me})$. For $R_g \to \infty$, an open circuit, the current is zero and with zero counter-torque, the shaft turns at the no-load speed. For a low value of R_g, at low speed where v_ω is small, relatively high current and torque will result. If R_g is too low, too much counter-torque will cause the propeller to stall.

The motor family of $T(\omega_{me})$ functions are linear and move away (with the same slope) from the origin as V_g increases. When generating, V_g becomes a variable dependent on the wind speed. The power source is mechanical for a generator and is considered here to be a speed source, in keeping with the model. The value of V_g can be determined from the no-load speed. A given wind speed corresponds to a value of ω_0, and from that, V_g can be calculated from the induced-voltage equation. Given the two generator parameters, then for a no-load wind speed of ω_0, a family of $T(R_g)$ curves results.

Charger Loading Optimization

A major goal of the wind system is to transfer maximum power from the wind to the converter output. According to the maximum power transfer theorem (see 'Maximum Power Transfer', p. 13), maximum power will be transferred from ω_s to R_g when the electrical impedance equals the mechanical impedance, R_{me}, referred to the electrical side as R_{me}', in series with the winding R;

$$R_g = R + R_{me}'$$

Consequently, the converter input should present a load of R_g to the generator at all times. To present an effective resistance of R_g at the generator terminals, consider the circuit shown below.

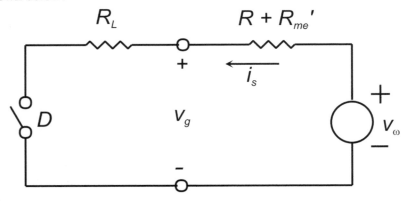

The duty ratio, D, of the load switch is varied from 0 to 1. During the on-time of the switching cycle, v_g is loaded with R_L, resulting in a current of v_g/R_L. During the off-time, the current is zero. The generator current, averaged over the switching cycle, T_s, is

$$\bar{i}_g = D \cdot \frac{v_\omega}{R + R_{me}' + R_L}$$

Applying the voltage-divider formula, the average generator terminal voltage is

$$\bar{v}_g = D \cdot v_\omega \cdot \left(\frac{R_L}{R + R_{me}' + R_L} \right) + (1 - D) \cdot v_\omega$$

$$= v_\omega \cdot \left(\frac{R_L + (1 - D) \cdot (R + R_{me}')}{R + R_{me}' + R_L} \right)$$

Then the effective R_g is based on the ratio of these averages:

$$R_g = \frac{\bar{v}_g}{\bar{i}_g} = \frac{R_L}{D} + \left(\frac{1 - D}{D} \right) \cdot (R + R_{me}')$$

For maximum power transfer, R_g is set equal to $R + R_{me}'$, resulting in the required D:

$$D = \frac{1}{2} \cdot \left(1 + \frac{R_L}{R + R_{me}'} \right)$$

For $R_L = R + R_{me}'$, then $D = 1$, which means that the switch is closed all the time. Alternatively, if $R_L = 0\ \Omega$, then $D = 0.5$, which is midrange, though the charger input resistance must be an ideal short. For practical design with a switching charger input, R_L must be in a range less than $R + R_{me}'$. As D increases, the effective R_g decreases.

For wind system design, choosing R_{me}' as a propeller parameter also affects D. As R_{me}' increases, the slope of the torque curve decreases, as shown in the T-ω_{me} plot on p. 92, until the value of D becomes small. For n-bit resolution of D, and a practical lower limit for R_L, the max-power R_g value can become resolution-limited. Consequently, a practical maximum is placed on the values of R_{me}'.

Wind Converter Circuits

At the other extreme, a small R_{me}' is desirable because this allows the wind to approach being an ideal speed source. At low speed, it is still capable of delivering high torque (and current, i_s) without stalling. However, in practice, R_{me}' will have a non-zero value, and this will limit the maximum current that can be obtained from the generator at low speed. For a given $Z_{me} = R_{me}$, the generator is constrained to follow the $T(\omega_{me})$ line down to zero torque (and current) as speed decreases. Voltage also decreases linearly with speed. Power increases by ω_{me}^2 and is maximum at the maximum speed the propellers can sustain before feathering or before the tip speed becomes supersonic.

Wind Generator Types

Wind generators can be any type of electric machine. Commercial units sometimes use synchronous generators with controlled field current, delivered through slip rings. These are the same type of machines sometimes used in larger engine-generator combinations. Control of the magnetic field allows the flux, λ_{me}, to be varied, as expressed in units of V/Hz me.

From the previous electric-machine modeling, with a fixed λ_{me}, operation at a given speed will produce an open-terminal output voltage of $v_o = \lambda_{me} \cdot (2 \cdot \pi \cdot f_{me})$ where f_{me} is the mechanical speed in Hertz. (60 rpm/Hz) If the electrical load increases, the engine must produce more torque to provide more output current at the same voltage. Yet neither constant-λ_{me} generators nor engines can change torque without also changing speed, causing the voltage to vary from a nominal 120 V rms.

To solve this problem, the field current of the generator is varied to change λ_{me} to keep the voltage constant while current varies. This is necessary when the generator output feeds directly into the load distribution wiring.

A variation on the induction motor found commonly in the more recent generators is to place diodes in series with windings on the rotor. These wound-rotor machines would otherwise behave as induction motors, but because of the rectifying of the rotor currents into pulsating unipolar currents, they have some of the characteristics of PMS machines, but without the magnets.

Wind Converter Requirements

A *wind converter* is an electronic power-system component placed between the wind generator and either the battery bank or HVDC bus. It must operate over a wide input voltage range while extracting maximum power from the source.

A minimalist approach to wind generator selection is to avoid slip rings for rotor control of λ_{me}, for slip rings are susceptible to wear-out and failure. By providing extra length to the power cable at the generator, it is free to swivel in its limited angular range with wind direction. It is just as well to avoid dc brush motors because of the periodic requirement to replace their brushes. The simplest and most reliable options are induction motors and permanent-magnet synchronous (PMS) or 'brushless dc' motors. Induction motors are readily available and lower in cost than PMS motors, mainly because they do not have costly magnets. They are also larger in size. They have a starting complication in that they need to be powered a little to start generating. This is because of the lack of a rotor field when not moving. Once a moving rotor field is established, the generator will provide its own field.

To generate an induced voltage in the stator windings, a rotor magnetic field as viewed from (or 'referred to') the stator that is changing in time is required, according to the basic flux relationship:

$$v = \frac{d\lambda}{dt} \approx \frac{\Delta\lambda}{\Delta t}$$

That is, the voltage induced in the stator windings is proportional to the rate of change of flux presented to them. The parameter relating the mechanical speed to the circuit-referred flux is λ_{me}.

PMS motors are a preferred choice though they cost more. They have higher power and torque density than induction motors and do not have any special starting requirement because the rotor field is from the magnets. PMS motors are increasingly available because of their wide use in automotive and HVAC applications, from alternator replacements to compressor and heat pump fan motors.

How large should a wind generator on a tower be? If the generator is too small, the cost of the tower is not justified. If it is too large, the tower must bear greater weight and becomes too expensive. An optimum homestead power output per tower is in the 1 to 3 kW range. In this range, steel poles hinged at the ground, with guy wires for lateral support, are not too expensive and can be readily maintained. Expect to take the generator and its aerodynamic components down a few times in the first installation. The PMS motor, with its higher power density, can generate more power per given supportable weight, making the power per tower higher for the same tower cost.

With the choice of a PMS motor for the generator, the motor parameters must be chosen to be within an optimum range. The key parameter is λ_{me}. To determine what it should be, start with wind-speed range estimation. Wind begins turning the propellers of most commercial units at about 5 to 7 mph. A ×15 wind-speed range, from 5 mph to 75 mph can be converted to metric units using some useful unit conversions:

$$1 \text{ km/h} = 0.6214 \cdot \text{mi/h} \; ; \; 1 \text{ m/s} = 0.4470 \cdot \text{mi/h} \, , \, \text{mph} = \text{mi/h}$$

This range is 3.1 to 46.6 km/h, or 2.24 to 33.53 m/s. A generator that outputs (open-circuit) 120 V rms, having an amplitude (peak) of 170 V at 3600 rpm (or 60 Hz mechanical) has $\lambda_{me} = 47.2$ V/krpm or 33.33 V rms/krpm. This is also equivalent to a flux of 0.45 V·s. The generator voltage range corresponding to wind-speed range is 10 V to 150 V rms or 14 V to 212 V peak. The output voltage of the wind converter is either 12 V or 24 V for battery charging (10 V to 15 V for a 12 V battery bank) or 170 V for

Wind Converter Circuits

the HVDC bus. A battery charging converter would have $V_o < V_g$ over essentially the entire range while for an HVDC converter, they would cross over about midrange.

Another consideration is that the input to the wind converter is a sine-wave, a bipolar waveform. If it is rectified to make it unipolar, then with a storage capacitor, it is input to the converter as static (dc) voltage. Or instead, the converter can have a power-factor controller (PFC) stage that converts a rectified sine-wave so that the generator is loaded resistively. A PFC controls input current, making the current waveform follow the voltage waveshape so that the difference between them is a scale factor, the input resistance. The amplitude of the controlled current is adjusted using a multiplier to regulate the output voltage. A PFC avoids a large storage capacitor. In the wind-generator power range, the PFC is the better alternative.

PFC circuits are often boost converters followed by a voltage-reducing converter such as a common-passive or 'buck' forward converter, in which the transformer reduces the voltage. We next look at the circuitry for wind converters.

Half-Bridge Driver

An attractive wind converter scheme is what I call the series-L zero-current-switching (ZCS) half-bridge converter. A *half-bridge* is simply half of a full- or H-bridge, with the other half replaced by a capacitive divider. The half-bridge driver consists of two active switches (an upper, S_U, and lower, S_L, switch) and two capacitors of equal value in series across from the switches, as shown below. The load connects through a transformer of primary inductance, L, to the center nodes of the two branches.

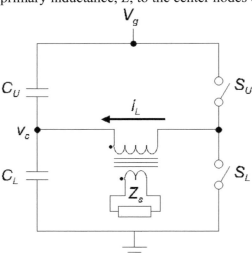

The question arises from past experience with this circuit whether the half-bridge will be stable, both for transformer flux and capacitor charge. In other words, does the transformer magnetizing current settle to a finite steady-state value? And does v_c also settle to a stable value?

Start with the static conditions for $C_U = C_L$. Then $V_c = V_g/2$. If the switches have equal duty-ratios - that is, they are on equal amounts of time - then the average voltage over a switching cycle applied to the transformer primary winding is also $V_g/2$, for half the time the switch center-node is connected to V_g and the other half to 0 V. In this equilibrium state, the average voltage across the primary winding is zero and the average current in it will become zero.

Now suppose that a disturbance of this symmetry occurs such that the upper switch remains on somewhat longer than the lower switch, and the average applied voltage at the switch center-node increases slightly. Then the average voltage across the transformer in a switching cycle is no longer 0 V, and current i_L will increase somewhat each cycle - a runaway flux situation. However, the non-zero offset in current is charging the capacitance at the center-node, causing its voltage to increase. Eventually, the increased voltage at v_c equals the average voltage at the switch center-node and the static (dc) component of i_L returns to zero. Flux imbalance ($V_p \neq 0$) causes charge imbalance between C_U and C_L that tends to restore flux balance. Similarly, if S_L stays on longer than S_U, then i_L decreases, and v_c decreases along with it. Both i_L and v_c will tend toward stable values so that flux balance and charge balance reinforce each other.

The capacitive side of the half-bridge can be represented by an equivalent circuit (using Thevenin's theorem) as shown below.

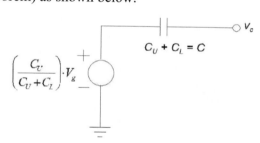

This equivalent capacitance of C forms a resonant circuit with the transformer inductance. The resonance has an impedance of

$$Z_n = \sqrt{\frac{L}{C}}$$

By reducing C or increasing L, the resonant impedance increases. If Z_n is made relatively large, then a relatively small change in i_C will cause a large change in v_C, thereby quickly correcting flux and charge imbalance. One method for achieving large Z_n in some half-bridge designs is to place a small-value capacitor in series with the primary winding. In effect, this reduces the equivalent capacitance. However, such a capacitor is redundant; C_U and C_L can be reduced to achieve the same effect provided that the smaller-valued capacitors can handle the required bridge current. Plastic capacitors are more expensive than electrolytic capacitors, and a single plastic capacitor in series with electrolytic C_U and C_L is lower in cost in some cases.

Additionally, by increasing Z_n, less series resistance is required to damp the resonance. The parasitic resistance in the primary circuit (switch r_{on}, winding resistance, capacitor ESR, interconnections) can be kept low and yet adequately damp a high-Z_n resonance. Consequently, by reducing C, increasing L, or both, half-bridge resonant damping increases.

Flux balance of the full-bridge driver (p. 71) involves essentially the same concept. The series capacitor size adjusts Z_n. Then Ohm's Law applied to a resonant circuit gives peak voltage,

$$\hat{v}_c = \hat{i} \cdot Z_n$$

Series-L ZCS Converter

The secondary series-L circuit with primary-side half-bridge driver is shown below. The equivalent circuit for the capacitive side of the half-bridge is shown.

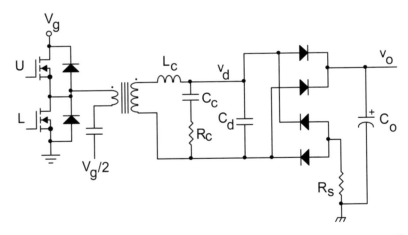

L_c is the series L. C_c, R_c are an RC snubber, the four diodes are a full-wave diode bridge, and C_d is their input capacitance, along with whatever other parasitic capacitance exists across the bridge input terminals.

The secondary winding leakage inductance is in series with L_c and adds to it. Together, they are L. Ordinarily, the snubber is required to damp the resonance formed by the leakage inductance and diode off-capacitance in a forward buck-derived converter. However, for the series-L circuit, the inductor is moved to the input side of the diode bridge. This seemingly minor change results in major differences in behavior, some very advantageous.

The upper (U) and lower (L) MOSFETs of the half-bridge are turned on and off in half-cycles, like the push-pull or full-bridge circuits explained previously. The on-time of U is designated here as t_{on+} and off-time is t_{off+}. Similarly, for the negative half-cycle when L is on, on- and off-times are t_{on-} and t_{off-}. During t_{off-} and t_{on+}, the secondary voltage, v_s, appears across the secondary winding as shown below, with dotted side of the winding positive. When the lower switch turns off and t_{off-} begins, current in L is flowing as shown in blue (dash), into the dotted terminal of the secondary winding.

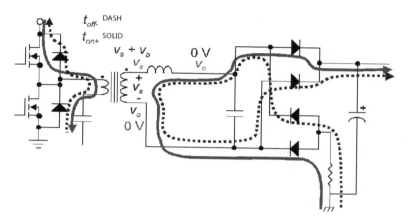

During this time, the right side of secondary inductance, L, is clamped to ground ($v_d = 0$ V) and the bottom of the secondary winding is clamped to V_o. The current in L induces a voltage into the primary winding, causing magnetizing current to continue to flow there, as shown. This magnetizing current flows through the upper diode, clamping the primary voltage to the supply. This maintains V_s across the secondary. If this decreasing current reaches zero within t_{off-}, then the secondary operates in DCM. If it does not become zero before t_{on+} begins, it is in CCM.

When the upper primary-side switch turns on, commencing t_{on+}, the polarity of v_s remains the same and (in CCM) opposes the current (dashed line) from the negative half-cycle. This current decreases and reverses, causing the diodes to switch their states, with the previously off (outer) pair now conducting, and the current in L reversed. This switching action of the diode bridge occurs at zero current in L, resulting in zero-power switching of the diodes. As shown in the lower text, voltage at the top of the secondary winding now drops to V_s, the bottom terminal of the winding is clamped to ground, and the bridge side of L is clamped to the output voltage, V_o. Because switching occurs at zero current in L, this minimizes excitation of any resonance involving L. Also, because all bridge diodes are involved in the switching, both nodes at the bridge input are always clamped, either to ground or the output, and v_r alternates between $\pm V_o$. The oscillograph for $V_s = 20$ V is shown below, with $V_o \cong V_s$ and duty ratio, $D \cong 1$. Trace 1 (upper) is the voltage at the top (dotted) terminal of the secondary winding. Trace 2 (lower) is the voltage at the right side of L.

Wind Converter Circuits

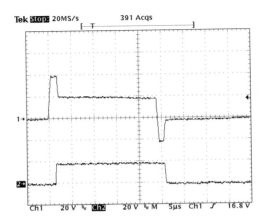

At the beginning of time division 2, t_{off-} begins as v_s reverses (to the polarity shown in the circuit above). Current flowing in L is now opposed by v_s, decays to zero, and reverses direction a third of a division later. The trace 1 voltage of $V_s + V_o = 40$ V. At this time, V_s falls to 20 V, and the trace 2 voltage (on the right side of L) rises from ground to V_o. The upper half-bridge switch turns on and t_{on+} begins during or after the 40 V pedestal. Because the clamp diode shunting the upper MOSFET is conducting, its turn-on is a zero-voltage (and hence zero-power) switching (ZVS) event.

When t_{on+} ends, t_{off+} begins at division 5.8 above, as shown below with a dashed line. The secondary voltage reverses, as shown, to maintain current flow and secondary current decays. During this time, magnetizing current continues to flow in the primary, clamping the primary voltage. The secondary current is constrained in value by L, and induces a voltage across the primary that keeps the (decaying) magnetizing current in the primary winding. It flows through the lower diode, clamping the top (dotted) end of the primary winding (and the primary winding voltage) to ground.

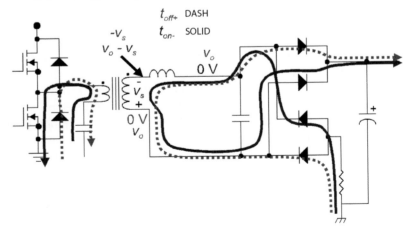

When t_{off+} ends, the lower MOSFET turns on (another ZVS event) and t_{on-} commences. This turn-on can occur during (CCM) or after (DCM) the $-V_s$ (-20 V) pedestal of trace 1.

When the secondary current reverses, then the top end of the secondary winding rises to $V_o - V_s$ volts as V_s opposes V_o at its bottom (undotted) terminal, shown in the lower trace (2) of the oscillograph below. The upper trace is the same as in the previous oscillograph; the lower trace shows the bottom terminal of the secondary winding changing from 0 V to $V_o = 20$ V as secondary current reverses polarity and begins to flow into the top terminal of the secondary winding.

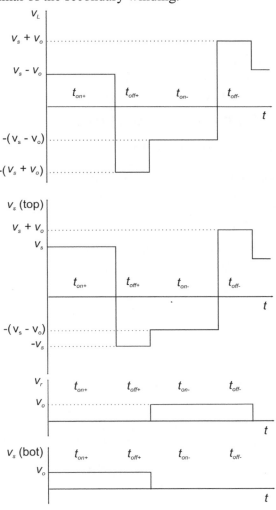

Wind Converter Circuits

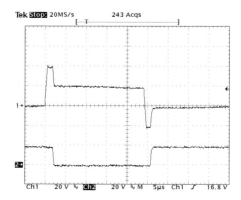

The oscillographs shown above were recorded with a resistive load with V_o close in value to V_s. A general voltage analysis of the converter results in the ideal waveforms, as shown here, where v_L is the voltage across L. (Left side of inductor is positive).

Series-L Current Waveform Analysis

At $V_o = 0$ V, the inductor current ramps up quickest, at a slope proportional to V_s, and ramps down slowest, at the same rate. As V_o is increased, the current up-slope decreases and is proportional to $V_s - V_o$. The magnitude of the down-slope increases, proportional to $V_s + V_o$. As V_o approaches V_s, the up-slope approaches zero and the down-slope approaches its maximum (negative) value of twice the value at $V_o = 0$ V. The positive half-cycle of the secondary current waveform, for both DCM and CCM, is shown below, where $\hat{i}_s$ is the peak secondary current.

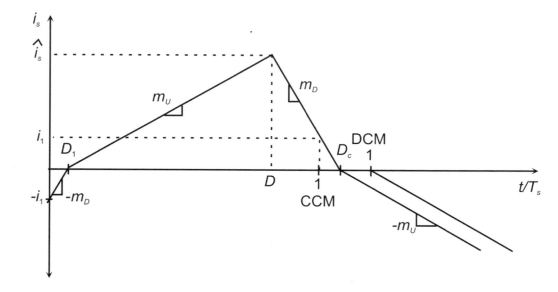

Now define

$$I_0 = \frac{V_s \cdot T_s}{L}$$

T_s is the switching period for half the primary switching cycle. The secondary voltage transfer function is

$$M = \frac{V_o}{V_s}$$

For a constant converter input voltage, V_g, then the secondary voltage will also be constant in amplitude, at V_s.

The on-time current slope, m_U, and off-time slope, m_D, can be expressed in the above parameters as

$$m_U = \frac{V_s - V_o}{L} \cdot T_s = I_0 \cdot (1 - M)$$

$$m_D = -\frac{V_s + V_o}{L} \cdot T_s = -I_0 \cdot (1 + M)$$

where the inductor on-time voltage,

$$V_{on} = V_s - V_o$$

During the off-time,

$$V_{off} = V_s + V_o$$

The peak current for the positive half-cycle can be expressed in either slope for both DCM and CCM;

Wind Converter Circuits

$$\hat{i}_s = m_U \cdot (D - D_1) = -m_D \cdot (D_c - D)$$
$$= I_0 \cdot (1 - M) \cdot (D - D_1) = I_0 \cdot (1 + M) \cdot (D_c - D)$$

where the *conduction duty ratio*, D_c, is the value of t/T_s when the secondary current becomes zero. For DCM, it stays at zero for the rest of the switching cycle; for CCM the negative half-cycle begins. Solving for D_c from the two peak-current expressions,

$$D_c = D + \frac{\hat{i}_s}{I_0} \cdot \frac{1}{1+M} = \begin{cases} \dfrac{2 \cdot D}{1+M}, \text{DCM} \\ D + \frac{1}{2} \cdot (1 - M), \text{CCM} \end{cases}$$

The two modes are distinguished by their values for D_1, the fraction of cycle time from its beginning until the positive half-cycle of current begins. By solving the two slope equations for D_1 instead,

$$D_1 = D - \frac{\hat{i}_s}{I_0} \cdot \frac{1}{1-M} = D_c - \frac{\hat{i}_s}{I_0} \cdot \frac{2 \cdot M}{(1+M) \cdot (1-M)} = \begin{cases} 0, \text{DCM} \\ -D_c', \text{CCM} \end{cases}$$

The DCM deadtime, $D_c' = 1 - D_c$, can be shifted to the beginning of the cycle so that one equation results for both modes. The DCM waveform is shifted along t/T_s to the right by $+D_c'$ so that the beginning of the up-ramp starts at $D_1 = +D_c'$. D has been shifted to $D + D_c'$ and D_c shifts to 1. The shifted slope expressions are

$$\hat{i}_s = m_U \cdot ((D + D_c') - D_c') = -m_D \cdot (1 - (D + D_c'))$$

These expressions reduce to the DCM equations.
   To solve for M from the above two expressions, use

$$-\frac{m_U}{m_D} = \frac{1-M}{1+M}$$

106

Then solving for $M(D, D_c)$ for both modes,

$$M = \frac{2 \cdot D - (D_c + D_1)}{D_c - D_1} = D_{eff} - D_{eff}'$$

where D is effectively

$$D_{eff} = \begin{cases} \dfrac{D}{D_c}, \text{DCM} \\ D + D_c', \text{CCM} \end{cases}$$

For DCM, $D_c' \geq 0$, and for CCM, $D_c' \leq 0$, as can be seen on the current waveform plot. $M(D_{eff})$ is linear with slope of 2 and is valid only for $\frac{1}{2} \leq D_{eff} \leq 1$, corresponding to $M \geq 0$. By applying

$$D - D' = 2 \cdot D - 1$$

the simplified expressions for M in both modes are

$$M(D, D_c) = \begin{cases} 2 \cdot \dfrac{D}{D_c} - 1, \text{DCM} \\ 2 \cdot (D + D_c') - 1, \text{CCM} \end{cases}$$

As a function of both D and D_c, M can be controlled by controlling both D and D_c: D by the half-bridge switches and D_c through control of f_s.

Peak Current

D_c in the above equations can be replaced by $\hat{i}_s$ so that M and D are expressed in peak current instead. The peak secondary current is, for the general case,

$$\hat{i}_s = m_U \cdot (D - D_1) = -m_D \cdot (D_c - D)$$

$$= \begin{cases} I_0 \cdot (1 - M) \cdot D = I_0 \cdot (1 + M) \cdot (D_c - D), \text{DCM} \\ \dfrac{I_0}{2} \cdot (1 - M) \cdot (1 + M) = \dfrac{I_0}{2} \cdot (1 - M^2), \text{CCM} \end{cases}$$

(Alternatively, $D_c - D = D' - D_c'$.) Substituting for D_c in the second DCM expression, the first expression results.

By solving the peak-current equation for M,

$$M(D, \hat{i}_s) = \begin{cases} 1 - \dfrac{\hat{i}_s / I_0}{D}, \text{DCM} \\ \sqrt{1 - 2 \cdot (\hat{i}_s / I_0)}, \text{CCM} \end{cases}$$

In CCM, $\hat{i}_s$ is unable to exceed $I_0/2$.

Average Current

The average secondary (and output) current is

$$\bar{i}_s = \begin{cases} \frac{1}{2} \cdot \hat{i}_s \cdot D_c, \text{DCM} \\ \frac{1}{2} \cdot \hat{i}_s, \text{CCM} \end{cases} = \begin{cases} I_0 \cdot \left(\dfrac{1 - M}{1 + M} \right) \cdot D^2, \text{DCM} \\ \dfrac{I_0}{4} \cdot (1 - M) \cdot (1 + M) = \dfrac{I_0}{4} \cdot (1 - M^2), \text{CCM} \end{cases}$$

For CCM, $\bar{i}_s$ is not dependent on D. The effect of D is to shift the phase of the current waveform in the switching cycle. As D increases, $D_c' < 0$ increases and the waveform half-cycle is increasingly shifted to the right, delayed until $i_1 = \hat{i}_s$ when $D = 1$. In CCM, secondary current is not controllable by D and is affected only by M.

Solving for D as a function of M in DCM, given $\bar{i}_s$ and f_s,

$$D(V_o) = D_0 \cdot \sqrt{\left(\dfrac{1 + v_o / V_s}{1 - v_o / V_s} \right)} = D_0 \cdot \sqrt{\dfrac{1 + M}{1 - M}}, \text{DCM}$$

where the duty ratio at zero output voltage is

$$D_0 \equiv D(0\,V) = \sqrt{\frac{L \cdot \bar{i}_s}{V_s \cdot T_s}} = \sqrt{\frac{\bar{i}_s}{I_0}}$$

The expression for $D(V_o)$ gives the value of D for a given average current.

The current equations can be solved for M, now expressed in parameter D_0 for fixed average-current;

$$M(D) = \begin{cases} \dfrac{D^2 - D_0^2}{D^2 + D_0^2}, \text{DCM} \\ \sqrt{1 - (2 \cdot D_0)^2} = M_{crit}, \text{CCM} \end{cases}$$

$M(D)$ is plotted for several values of D_0. Above M_{crit}, D no longer causes M to increase for a given $\bar{i}_s$. A larger M would require less average current. The fixed $\bar{i}_s$ constrains the upper range of M.

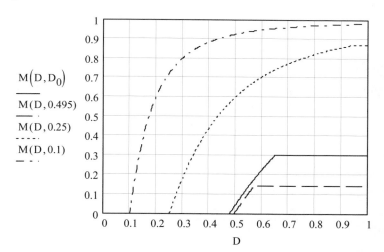

$$\begin{array}{l} \mathrm{M}(\mathrm{D}, \mathrm{D_0}) \\ \overline{\mathrm{M}(\mathrm{D}, 0.495)} \\ \overline{\mathrm{M}(\mathrm{D}, 0.25)} \\ \text{-----} \\ \mathrm{M}(\mathrm{D}, 0.1) \\ \text{-- -} \end{array}$$

Voltage control lets the current be free to vary to achieve a given V_o. The plots of $\bar{i}_s(V_o)/I_0$ with D as parameter are given below. Note that $\bar{i}_s(D, M) = \bar{i}_s(1, 0) = I_0$; $\bar{i}_s(1, 1) = 0$ A. As D exceeds 0.5, the current follows the CCM plot to intersect at higher values of M_{crit}.

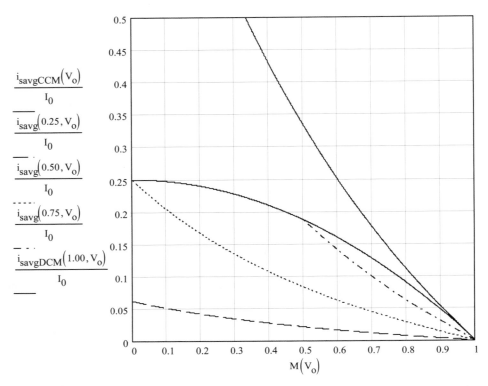

RMS Current

The rms current expression in DCM or in CCM (for which D_c is set to 1) is

$$\tilde{i}_s = \sqrt{\frac{D_c}{3}} \cdot \hat{i}_s$$

The *form factor*, $\kappa_s = \tilde{i}_s / \bar{i}_s$, is the ratio of power loss caused by ohmic heating (rms current) per desired (average) current - a power-waveform 'figure of demerit'. The triangular current waveform has a minimum $\kappa_s = 2/\sqrt{3} \approx 1.15$ that increases with M and decreases with D in DCM;

$$\kappa_s = \frac{\tilde{i}_s}{\bar{i}_s} = \frac{2}{\sqrt{3}} \cdot \frac{1}{\sqrt{D_c}} \cong \frac{1.155}{\sqrt{D_c}}$$

κ_s cannot be less than one, nor can the peak/average ratio. In CCM, $\kappa_s \approx 1.155$ and $D_c = 1$ in the expression for κ_s, plotted below.

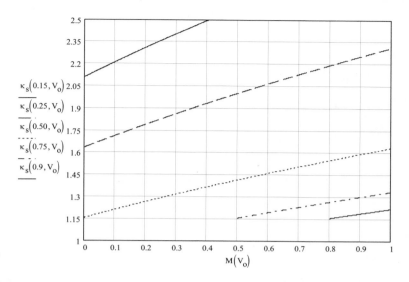

DCM/CCM Boundary

The boundary between the CCM and DCM regions occurs at minimum CCM at which $D_c = 1$. The value of D under this condition is

$$D_{crit} = D(D_c = 1) = \tfrac{1}{2} \cdot \left(1 + M_{crit}\right)$$

$$M_{crit} = \sqrt{1 - (2 \cdot D_0)^2} \; , D_0 \leq \tfrac{1}{2}$$

If D_0 exceeds 1/2, the converter will operate only in CCM. D, D_c, and D_{crit} are plotted below against M for the following parameters:

$$V_s = 165 \text{ V}; L = 470 \text{ } \mu\text{H}; T_s = 25 \text{ } \mu\text{s}; \bar{i}_s = 2 \text{ A}$$

$D_0 \approx 0.477$ and $M_{crit} \approx 0.3$. CCM occurs for $M \geq M_{crit}$. In CCM, M is independent of D and the DCM plot of D is not valid above D_{crit}.

Operation deep within DCM ($D_c \ll 1$) can result in excessive peak current and occurs when D_0 is too small. When D_0 is too large, then the required current cannot be obtained for the upper part of the desired M operating range.

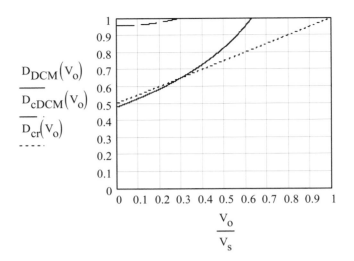

$$\frac{D_{DCM}(V_o)}{D_{cDCM}(V_o)}$$

$$\overline{D_{cr}(V_o)}$$

- - - - ·

$$\frac{V_o}{V_s}$$

Maximum Output Power

The optimal operating point for this converter may be taken to be where maximum power transfer occurs. Average output power, $V_o \cdot \bar{i}_s$, is maximum when the converter operates at

$$M(P_{max}) = M_{opt} = \begin{cases} \sqrt{2} - 1 \cong 0.414 \text{ , DCM} \\ 1/\sqrt{3} \cong 0.577 \text{ , CCM} \end{cases}$$

as shown on the plots below. These plots are of average output power, normalized by dividing by $V_s \cdot I_0$. The CCM has only one plot because average current is fixed in CCM. It is also the plot with the greatest maximum power, at a value of $M = 0.577$ slightly greater than the 0.5 of the maximum power-transfer theorem (which applies to linear circuits). For $D > \frac{1}{2}$, P_{max} occurs at the DCM/CCM boundary if M_{crit} is below CCM $M(P_{max})$. $\bar{i}_s$ (DCM) intersects $\bar{i}_s$ (CCM) at CCM $M(P_{max})$ with a D value of

$$D_{opt} = \sqrt{\frac{1}{6} \cdot \frac{\sqrt{3}+1}{\sqrt{3}-1}} = \frac{1}{2} \cdot \left(1 + \frac{1}{\sqrt{3}}\right) \cong 0.789$$

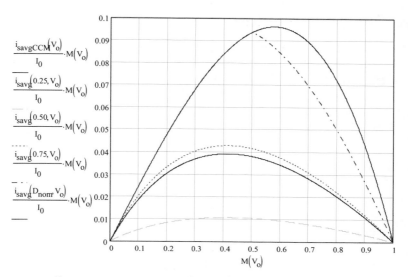

The corresponding average current values at P_{max} are

$$\bar{i}_s(P_{max}) = \bar{i}_{sopt} = \begin{cases} I_0 \cdot D^2 \cdot (\sqrt{2}-1) \cong (0.414) \cdot I_0 \cdot D^2 \text{ , DCM} \\ \dfrac{I_0}{4} \cdot \dfrac{2}{3} = \dfrac{I_0}{6} \cong (0.167) \cdot I_0 \text{ , CCM} \end{cases}$$

By operating with D control in DCM near the DCM/CCM boundary of P_{max}, maximum power is transferred for the operating point:

$$V_s = V_o/(0.577) = (1.732) \cdot V_o$$
$$D = 0.789$$
$$\bar{i}_s = I_0/6$$

These values result in the theoretical maximum power transfer that can be achieved as a standard of comparison to actual converter designs and implementations. Non-zero design margins require operating at somewhat less than the optimum, with some margin inside DCM. Alternatively, operation within CCM for a given average output current has the advantage of primary-switch ZVS at turn-on.

For low values of V_o, the output resistance is relatively high, making this converter less prone to failure from output shorts.

Series-L Design Procedure

The above derivations have been given to provide deeper insight into the following design procedure, derived from them. Specific design values are given in the procedure as examples that correspond to the above plots.

1. Choose switching frequency, $f_s = 40$ kHz, and nominal (midrange) output voltage, $V_{onom} = 450$ V. Then $T_s = 1/f_s = 25$ μs.

$$M_{opt} = \frac{1}{\sqrt{3}} \approx 0.5774$$

and

$$V_{sopt} = \frac{V_{onom}}{M_{opt}} = 779.42 \text{ V}$$

2. Choose the secondary voltage amplitude, V_s to be near the optimum value, based on other factors such as the transformer turns ratio. Let $V_s = 825$ V. Then converter secondary-side voltage gain is

$$M = \frac{V_o}{V_s}$$

Because V_s is now fixed, M is another way of expressing V_o.

3. Choose the nominal average output current, $\bar{i}_s = 2$ A. Let this be the optimal value of $\bar{i}_s$. Then

$$I_0 = 6 \cdot \bar{i}_s = 12 \text{ A} \Rightarrow I_0/4 = 3 \text{ A}$$

4. Calculate the value of L. The optimal value is

$$L_{opt} = \frac{V_{sopt} \cdot T_s}{I_0} = 1.624 \text{ mH}$$

Because we chose to adjust the value of V_s from the optimum, V_{sopt}, then for the chosen V_s, the value of

$$L = \frac{V_s \cdot T_s}{I_0} = 1.719 \, \text{mH}$$

5. In DCM operation, nominal

$$D_0(\text{DCM}) = \sqrt{\frac{\bar{i}_s}{I_0}} = 0.4082$$

The DCM conduction duty-ratio is the fraction of T_s that is the non-zero-current time;

$$D_c(\text{DCM}) = \frac{2 \cdot D}{1 + M}$$

The nominal duty-ratio is

$$D = D_0 \cdot \sqrt{\frac{1 + V_{onom}/V_s}{1 - V_{onom}/V_s}} = 0.7528$$

CCM does not allow control of V_o with D and is at the upper end of the range of operation, where the optimal D occurs, at

$$D_{opt} = \sqrt{\frac{1}{6} \cdot \frac{1 + M_{opt}}{1 - M_{opt}}} = 0.7887$$

DCM/CCM boundary: the critical (boundary) value of D is

$$D_{crit} = \tfrac{1}{2} \cdot (1 + M)$$

6. The value of M at the boundary is

$$M_{crit} = \sqrt{1-(2\cdot D_0)^2}$$

7. Though not derived previously, the incremental or small-signal transfer function of $V_o(D)$ is

$$\frac{\Delta V_o}{\Delta D} \approx \frac{dV_o}{dD} = \frac{4\cdot D}{D^2 + \dfrac{\bar{i}_s(\text{DCM})}{I_0}} = 4.106$$

This procedure has resulted in design values for the main parameters of the series-L converter. The peak and rms currents can then be calculated from them;

$$\hat{i}_s(\text{DCM}) = I_0 \cdot (1-M)\cdot D$$

$$\tilde{i}_s = \begin{cases} \sqrt{\dfrac{D_c(\text{DCM})}{3}}\cdot \hat{i}_s \,, & M \le M_{crit} \\[2ex] \dfrac{\hat{i}_s}{\sqrt{3}} \,, & M > M_{crit} \end{cases}$$

Inductance Moved to Primary Circuit

A variation on the series-L converter is to place the series inductance in the primary loop. L_c can be referred to the primary as $n^2{\cdot}L_c$. This circuit has the advantage of requiring (for $n > 1$) an inductor with a lower current rating by $1/n$, though the inductance value is larger by n^2. Inductance varies with turns-squared and no reduction in power loss from parasitic resistance is gained. However, there is a disadvantage; the magnetizing current of the transformer also flows through L_c and if significant can make the inductor larger than what it would be on the secondary side. Magnetizing current can be reduced by increasing the magnetizing inductance, resulting in more primary turns and a larger transformer. This is avoided with the secondary series-L.

Series-L Performance Evaluation

The placement of L_c before the diode bridge instead of after it (as in a conventional full-wave-bridge-secondary forward converter) has several advantages:

Secondary resonance and snubber damping resistor losses are reduced in DCM or eliminated in CCM;

The bridge diodes are ZCS and have negligible switching loss;

The primary-side power switches are ZVS at turn-on in CCM, with no turn-on loss;

Inherent current limiting occurs at the output.

The choice of the L_c design value must be large enough to keep maximum secondary current to within design bounds. It must raise the impedance that loads the secondary winding so that with a shorted output, secondary current is not excessive. It also must not be made too large or else secondary (and output) current will not be sufficient over the desired input voltage range. When designed within this range, the converter has an inherent immunity to failure due to output shorts. Optimal L_c is calculated from the optimal I_0 for a given V_o.

Maximum power is delivered at $V_s = \sqrt{3} \cdot V_o$. The series-L power calculation is somewhat involved but is easiest to carry out at the mode boundary where $D_1 = 0$ and $D = D_{crit}$. The waveform of v_s during the positive current half-cycle is a bipolar square-wave, with amplitude V_s during D and $-V_s$ during D'. The current is a triangle-wave with an average value of $\bar{i}_s = \bar{i}_o$ for both D and D' intervals. Then calculating average power directly from Watt's Law,

$$\bar{P}_{scrit} = (V_s \cdot \bar{i}_o) \cdot D_{opt} + (-V_s) \cdot (\bar{i}_o) \cdot D_{opt}' = (V_s \cdot \bar{i}_o) \cdot (2 \cdot D_{opt} - 1)$$

$$= (\sqrt{3} \cdot V_o \cdot \bar{i}_o) \cdot \left(2 \cdot \left[\frac{1}{2} \cdot \left(1 + \frac{1}{\sqrt{3}} \right) \right] - 1 \right) = V_o \cdot \bar{i}_o$$

This calculation merely confirms that no power is dissipated in the ideal series-L secondary circuit. It does not, however, tell us what power rating the transformer must have. To find this quantity, the rms secondary voltage and current are first derived as follows.

$$\tilde{v}_s = \sqrt{D \cdot V_s^2 + D' \cdot (-V_s)^2} = V_s \cdot \sqrt{D - D'}$$

At the mode boundary, $D = D_{crit}$. Substituting,

$$\tilde{v}_{scrit} = V_s$$

Triangle-wave rms current is

Wind Converter Circuits

$$\tilde{i}_s = \frac{\hat{i}_s}{\sqrt{3}} = \frac{2}{\sqrt{3}} \cdot \bar{i}_s = \frac{2}{\sqrt{3}} \cdot \bar{i}_o$$

Then for the optimal values,

$$\bar{p}_{xfmrcrit} = 2 \cdot \sqrt{D_{opt}} \cdot (V_o \cdot \bar{i}_o) = \sqrt{2 \cdot \left(1 + \frac{1}{\sqrt{3}}\right)} \cdot (V_o \cdot \bar{i}_o) \cong 1.776 \cdot \bar{p}_o$$

The series-L diode voltage utilization for the optimal (p_{max}) operating point is one (V_o across off diodes), and the current utilization is 0.5. Then the power utilization of the secondary diodes is 0.5.

The series-L secondary current is all ripple current with an output amplitude of half the peak. In an application such as a battery charger, this large ac current is irrelevant, and the ripple might even be considered an advantage for lead-acid battery desulfonation. The series-L topology is optimal for high R_{out} (high voltage, low current) applications, though it can be competitive with voltage-reducing converters. The optimal M of $1/\sqrt{3} \approx 0.577$ reduces output voltage but with the disadvantage (unlike a transformer or the forward converter) of not proportionately increasing output current.

Peak current control of output voltage appears simplest because the converter gain (with D) in DCM remains constant with V_o. Control of V_o using D with a constant-current load poses the greatest difficulty for control because of the nonlinearity of gain with D.

An advantage of this initially complicated topology for efficiency is the low current form factor (rms/avg), about 1.155 in CCM. At $D_c = 1$ (minimum CCM), a 16 % increase of rms-to-average current is quite acceptable, while a peak/average ratio of $2/D_c$ (or ≤ 2 in CCM) is well within the bounds of diodes and transistors. At worst case ($V_o = 0$ V) with a minimum D of 40 %, peak/average current is 5, still within semiconductor range. This current waveform is at the switching frequency, making the duration of the peaks small relative to switch thermal response times. A disadvantage of this scheme is the peak-to-average ratio of the secondary current. Because inductor current is bipolar (ac) and triangular, peak current will always be at least twice the average.

Another disadvantage is that with bipolar inductor current, the inductor has to be designed using high-frequency switching materials (ferrites). Consequently, the inductor will be somewhat larger and costlier. However, this disadvantage is minimal compared to the relatively small inductance value, the increase in efficiency due to zero-power switching, low current form factor, and no dissipative secondary damping. The exception is the primary switches at turn-off, which still produce a primary resonance. It can be damped with a low-power series RC across the primary winding.

The series-L ZCS converter is appealing to consider for use wherever a voltage reduction is involved, as an alternative to the forward buck-derived converter. The wind converter is a prime possibility as are off-line battery chargers. Although the analysis is more complicated than the simpler converter types, once understood, the series-L converter can offer higher efficiency without any substantial disadvantages. It is worth adding to the off-grid power converter library of circuits.

Load Power Supplies

In power-grid-driven systems, minor attention is usually given to home loads. In an off-grid system, however, to what the plug connects the electric source is of greater concern. In both cases, some form of 120 V ac (or 240 V ac in Europe and elsewhere) is present. Motors and lights that are driven directly from the distribution line present loading characteristics covered in other chapters. For equipment with power supplies - usually electronic equipment - two factors raise interest in the kind of power supply the load has. First, what effect will a power waveform other than sine-wave have on it; and second, is it possible to run this device on dc instead? This second consideration opens the possibility of abandoning inverters, or reducing their use, and distributing 170 V dc, making the HVDC system bus the load distribution system.

Transformer Input Supplies

Older equipment with 50 or 60 Hz transformers have a typical power input circuit as shown below.

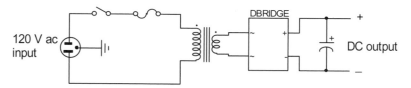

For this type of equipment, there is no hope of operation from a dc bus. The transformer is an inherently ac device and windings driven by dc are simply wire shorts. Replacement of the 60 Hz supply with a switcher is one option. For small equipment, a wall-mount switcher can supply low-voltage dc and connect into the dc output port of the 60 Hz supply.

For 60 Hz bipolar square-wave power distribution, the higher harmonics of the square-wave will pass through the transformer, increasing power loss with frequency. Expect ac-operated devices such as 60 Hz transformers and motors to dissipate somewhat more power under square-wave drive. However, the efficiency of a 60 Hz supply, as that shown above, might actually improve with square-wave drive because the square-wave peak lasts much longer than a sine-wave peak. The secondary circuit consists of a full-wave diode bridge followed by a storage capacitor, to provide relatively constant voltage. This peak-charging scheme has the disadvantage that the rectifier bridge diodes turn on only when the rectified sine-wave output of the bridge is greater in voltage than that of the capacitor plus diode on-voltages. This time is short and occurs around the peak of the sine-wave. During this short time, all the charge needed to produce the output current during the cycle must be delivered to the capacitor. If the diode bridge conducts for 5 % of the rectified-sine cycle, it must deliver current 20 times (1/0.05) the average supply output current. Current spikes have a high *crest factor*:

$$\text{Crest factor} = \frac{\hat{x}}{\tilde{x}}$$

High crest-factor waveforms cause electrical noise and reduce the efficiency of power systems; they are highly undesirable yet unavoidable in this simple type of input circuit. A square-wave peak lasts for about half of each half-cycle and needs to deliver only about twice the average current during conduction. This causes less power to be lost in the diodes and capacitor, and also in the transformer.

Switching Supplies

Switching converters omit the large, heavy, and expensive 60 Hz transformer and usually rectify the power line input directly with a circuit like that of the secondary circuit used by the 60 Hz supply. The difference is that the output will be (for 120 V rms) the peak value of the power-line voltage, or 170 V. This voltage is the input to the converter switching circuit.

The switcher peak-charging input circuit still has the high crest factor. Furthermore, when conduction occurs, it is into a capacitance and the input of the supply appears capacitive (reactive) to the source. The peak-charging circuit is increasingly being replaced by a power-factor controller (PFC) circuit. This is a circuit that has a similarity to the maximum-input-power circuits of solar and wind chargers in that it controls its own input impedance. A PFC circuit causes the input of the supply to appear resistive to the power outlet instead of capacitive. It does this by controlling the input current and making the current waveform be the same in shape as the input voltage waveform. This makes the current in-phase with the voltage. If the current at each point in time is some scale-factor of the voltage, then by Ohm's Law, the scale factor is simply $I_{in}/V_{in} = 1/R_{in}$, where R_{in} is the input resistance, not reactance.

A PFC supply input, like a typical non-PFC switching supply, can operate on a wide range of line voltages and either an ac or dc waveform of nearly any waveshape. Most equipment, including consumer entertainment equipment of the last two decades and CFLs, use switching supplies, sometimes in their own enclosure as wall-mount or desktop units. If all loads are of this type, then a HVDC distribution system becomes feasible and the inverter component of the power system is eliminated, except for motors such as in water pumps, fans, shavers, and refrigerator compressors.

Supply Fans

Some supplies have fans for cooling. These fans are almost always axial box fans and run on low-voltage dc. Large supply fans that run on the power line almost always contain their own ac-to-dc conversion and can operate from 170 V dc. Auxiliary loads other than the power supply itself, such as power indicator lights, are sometimes driven directly from the (switched and fused) power line in older equipment. Be aware of such considerations for dc operation.

CFL Supplies

Compact fluorescent lamps have built-in lamp drivers that are high-voltage inverters. The supply for these inverters is usually simple diode-bridge voltage-doubler circuits. These circuits are also peak-charging. What is worse, the load presented to them is resonant. A series resonant circuit appears inductive above the resonant frequency and capacitive below it. This can cause instability in inverter control circuits. (See 'Inverter Load Instability' in *Your own Eco-Electrical Home Power System.*) The load impedance is referred through the inverter stage to the battery or other source converter and is one of the functional blocks in its feedback loop. In effect, a resonant circuit has been placed in the loop. A lightly damped resonance has a quick change of delay with frequency, making it difficult to stabilize the loop. Ideally, the dc source for the inverter should be isolated from the indeterminate loading of the inverter. One method, though somewhat costly, is to add an LC filter at the output of the inverter, to make the loading impedance that the inverter drives be less variable.

On the leading edge of fluorescent driver development are μC-based drivers. The Atmel AVR-series μC (AT90PWM2B) was designed for this application. It has two PWM outputs. One is for a PFC input stage which eliminates the inverter-converter stability problem. The other drives the FL half-bridge with a PWMed sine-wave, for lower electrical noise from lighting. The circuit details of CFL inverters are in the 'Fluorescent Lamps' chapter.

Fluorescent Lamps

Incandescent lamps are joining CRTs on their way to obsolescence while compact fluorescent lamps (CFLs) and white LEDs are dominating lighting. Like all electronics, CFL lamp drivers eventually fail. Descrying the throw-away mentality and with the requisite skills already in hand (or head), the home-electric user can consider the practice of CFL repair. Happily, this is not usually difficult.

Fluorescent Lamp Electrical Model

Both tubular and compact fluorescent lamps (CFLs) operate on the same principle. A small amount of mercury is present in the tube and some of it will exist as a vapor. When a sufficiently strong electric field occurs across the electrode ends of the tube (whether straight, coiled, or bent), free electrons in the low-pressure tube are accelerated and an effect like that of avalanche (zener) diodes occurs. Mercury ions are accelerated by the field and in colliding with other mercury atoms, ionize them, until an ionized stream or arc exists between electrodes. This arc then conducts and is self-sustaining, heating and producing ions. Mercury is a low-melting-point metal that conducts electricity well and despite its toxicity is used because it works in this application like no other readily-available material. Thus, one disadvantage of fluorescent lighting is the contamination caused by broken florescent bulbs. Disposal of worn-out lamps is another consideration.

Once an arc is struck, the electrical behavior of the lamp changes from a low capacitance to a relatively low resistance with an operating voltage that is usually 5 to 10 times lower than the strike voltage. The lamp thus has two modes: lit and unlit. The lamp driver must provide the required drive waveforms to the lamp terminals for both, and this complicates fluorescent (and also high-intensity discharge, or HID) lamp driver design. High voltage, low current drive is followed by lower-voltage, higher-current drive. It is as though the driver needs to 'shift gears' in output resistance, and with a fixed turns-ratio transformer in the driver, this is not trivial. Yet driver circuits can be fit into the tight compartments at the base of CFLs.

The unlit FL model is a capacitance of tens of picofarads. The lit equivalent electrical circuit is more complex and is called the Mader-Horn FL model, after its FL researchers. It is shown below.

Fluorescent Lamps

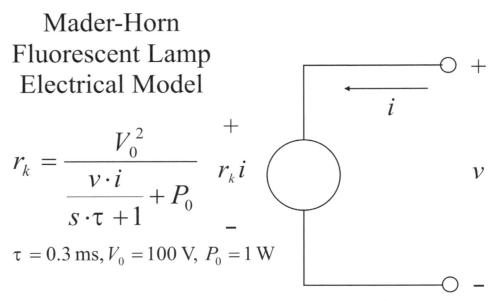

Mader-Horn Fluorescent Lamp Electrical Model

$$r_k = \frac{V_0^2}{\dfrac{v \cdot i}{s \cdot \tau + 1} + P_0}$$

$$\tau = 0.3 \text{ ms}, V_0 = 100 \text{ V}, P_0 = 1 \text{ W}$$

The model is simply the FL terminal resistance, r_k, a nonlinear resistance that describes the v-i characteristics of FLs when lit. The r_k equation, with typical parametric values, is

$$r_k = \frac{V_0^2}{\dfrac{v \cdot i}{s \cdot \tau + 1} + P_0} \quad , \tau = 0.3 \text{ ms}, V_0 = 100 \text{ V}, P_0 = 1 \text{ W}$$

The $s \cdot \tau + 1$ in the denominator is recognized by engineers as a *pole*. Up to a *break frequency* of $f_p = 2 \cdot \pi / \tau \approx 21$ kHz, $(s \cdot \tau + 1)$ has an aspproximate value of one. Above f_p, the FL power, $v \cdot i$, is effectively decreased in value in the equation in proportion to frequency. The pole shows that the FL has a time-dependent or *dynamic* response in that lamp resistance, r_k, takes a little time - about $5 \cdot \tau = 1.5$ ms - to decrease to its steady-state value. Under operation below f_p, including steady-state operation for which the frequency variable, $s = 0$ Hz, then the lamp resistance simplifies to

$$r_k = \frac{V_0^2}{v \cdot i + P_0} \quad , V_0 = 100 \text{ V}, P_0 = 1 \text{ W}$$

It is plotted below for steady-state operation.

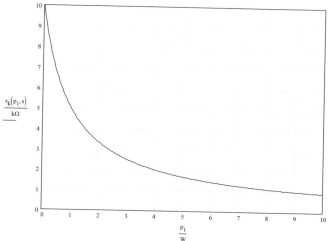

The circuit model for a lit FL operating at rated power is approximated by a current source if the power, $v \cdot i$, is kept constant. (High-intensity lamps, or HIDs, such as sodium-vapor lamps, are approximated instead by a voltage source when lit.) Equivalent circuits for lit and unlit FL lamps are shown below.

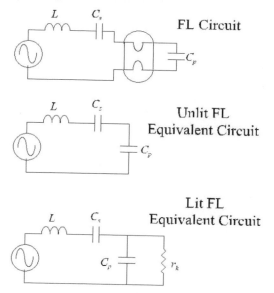

From the above plot, r_k for near-constant current is in the 1 kΩ range.

FL drivers must be able to generate the high strike voltage across unlit lamps. When unlit, the series (C_s) and parallel (C_p) capacitances form an equivalent capacitance smaller than either. This series-C of value,

Fluorescent Lamps

$$C = \frac{C_s \cdot C_p}{C_s + C_p}$$

resonates at a relatively high frequency with the series L. C_p provides a heater-current path yet cannot be made too large, for the strike voltage must occur across it. C_p thus forms a capacitive divider with C_s, and in the unlit state, has a typical value of about $C_s/10$. C_s thus looks like a short and the resonant frequency is determined largely by the FL capacitance in parallel with C_p, where C_p is larger, to provide heater current. FLs that do not need the C_p path for heater current might need it to establish the optimal capacitance across the tube. By dominating over a range of smaller FL capacitance values, the sum of the two capacitances is reduced in range by C_p.

Once lit, the tube resistance, r_k, dominates and C_p becomes a high impedance shunting it. The lit-FL circuit is approximately a series LCR (L, C_s, r_k). Then the resonant frequency decreases from the unlit state and is largely determined by L and C_s. The lower frequency also causes the reactance of C_p to be higher than before, essentially removing it from the circuit.

Obsolete FL drivers are large inductors, or 'ballasts', placed in series with the lamp and power line. At power-line frequencies, a large (and bulky) inductor is required. The change in voltage across the inductor with changing current raises the lamp voltage to where it will strike. This can be assisted by preheating the electrodes so that they more readily emit electrons. Lamps with heaters are called 'rapid-start' and those without are called 'instant-start'. Heated lamps require a 'starter' which heats the filaments for some time, then turns them off after the lamp has lit.

The preferred driver for off-line (120 V or 240 V ac) CFLs is the *half-bridge* circuit, as shown below. A *bridge* circuit generates a bipolar waveform across a load from a

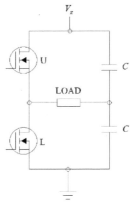 single (usually positive) supply. The rectified line voltage, V_g, is applied across the load, left end positive, when transistor switch, U, is on. When L is on instead (carefully avoiding having both U and L on at the same time!), then the load polarity is reversed. The two divider capacitors forming the right branch of the bridge circuit establish $V_g/2$ on the right terminal of the load. The load therefore is driven by a voltage of $\pm V_g/2$. The capacitive divider does not always appear in FL driver circuits as shown in this idealized half-bridge.

FLs can be operated from a constant (dc) voltage but it highly reduces operating life. Consequently, all practical FL drivers generate a bipolar (ac) waveform, preferably sinusoidal. The half-bridge driver is usually made part of an oscillator circuit in CFLs using multi-winding transformers to provide gate or base drive from the output current.

An optimal CFL circuit has evolved and all of the CFLs I have dissected have similar circuits. They will now be examined in the context of repair while noting their design features.

CFL Driver Repair

Shown below is a CFL that was repaired and operating on the electronics bench.

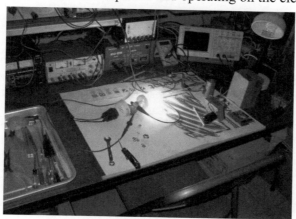

The specialized item for CFL repair is the power cord with a lamp socket, shown in the picture. This is a handy power-line adapter for work on any device that screws into a lamp bulb socket. The non-specialized but necessary item is the *line conditioning unit*, at minimum an isolation transformer, augmented by a variac, circuit breaker, and power switch, for 'smoke testing' power circuits gracefully.

One of the most difficult aspects of fixing a CFL is to open the enclosure. They snap apart at the seam, as shown in the close-up photo below. The upper section is the lower part of the enclosure, viewed from the end of the T1 bulb base. The soldered contact is cratered a bit from desoldering one of the two wires that connect to the base. The lower part consists of the CFL, upper enclosure, and inverter electronics board. Midway along the enclosure rim there is a notch. CFLs can be hard to open and might require wedging a screwdriver into the seam and rotating. Find where the snaps themselves are and pry at those locations. Substantial force in prying apart obstinate enclosures is sometimes needed. Be careful when doing such prying, to avoid breaking the fluorescent bulb - that bulb with some mercury in it. (However, it is better to fix the electronics and continue to use the bulb than relegate both to the dump.)

Fluorescent Lamps

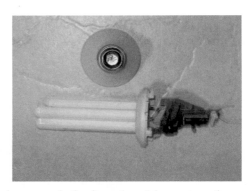

Once the enclosure is opened, the board and lamp together pull out from the base, as shown for the smaller CFL below. Usually repair can be effected without further disassembly, though you might want to unsolder the two power-line connections to the base to free the board for more careful examination of the circuitry. One wire is at the bottom and is unsoldered from the outside; the other is at the side near the edge of the outer metal screw-connector. These are easy to resolder later and (unlike too much newer technology) can be resoldered multiple times without destroying the connector.

The CFL lamp has four wires connected to it which can also be unsoldered. But don't end up with the wires connected to the board, as shown in this photo. They should be unsoldered on the board side to remove the lamp. (This inverter was saved from a unit with a broken CFL lamp.) Reassembly reverses the disassembly procedure. Be sure to form a smooth but sizeable hump of solder on the bottom of the connector base so that it contacts the prong in the socket when screwed into a lighting fixture.

The inverters of several CFLs were found to have the same basic circuit in all of them, regardless of brand or power rating. All use a half-bridge driving a series-resonant circuit. Despite the prevalence of MOSFET power switches in much of today's electronics, high-voltage NPN BJTs were used in the examined CFLs. Two magnetics components were used: the base driver, and the output inductor that forms a series resonance with the CFL capacitance.

The circuit of a 9 W CFL inverter (possibly Matsui) for 120 V ac use is shown below. This CFL circuit illustrates some typical features. The MJE13000-series BJTs are common in CFLs. They are high-volume, high-voltage bipolar junction transistors

(BJTs) in TO-92 or TO-225 packages. In this application, power is delivered at high impedance and low currents make it possible to use these BJTs.

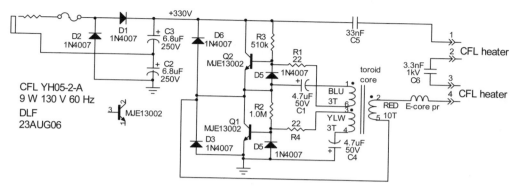

This design uses a peak-charging full-wave voltage doubler for the supply. In the particular unit from which this circuit was traced, one of the supply capacitors (C2, C3) failed. The most likely failed parts are the transistors and then the supply electrolytic capacitors. Usually, a failure of either will result in overcurrent, causing the on-board fuse to blow. These fuses are probably intended for system-level power-distribution safety because they usually do not protect whatever components in the inverter are vulnerable. The transistors work as well as the fuse in protecting the power line. Consequently, without a replacement fuse, several alternatives that will probably work just as well are: a small-diameter fusible wire, segment of solder, or small snap-in fuse with leads soldered onto the ends.

The half-bridge is self-oscillating with transformer base drive. For the required static (dc) turn-on current, current from R2 (through R3) turns Q1 on, current increases in Q1 from out of the +330V supply, into pin 1 of the CFL bulb, back out of pin 4 and through the series inductor, through pins 2 and 5 (the primary winding) of the gate-drive transformer, inducing a voltage across the secondary drive winding of pins 3 and 4. The base drive to Q1 is thus sustained dynamically, and the low-output-level half-cycle of oscillation is underway. As base current from the transformer sustains Q1 conduction, C4 is charged by that current and eventually its decreasing voltage (on the negative terminal) is sufficient to shut off Q1. The decreasing current of its turn-off causes the secondary base-drive winding with pins 6 and 1 to turn on Q2 and the positive half-cycle begins. Note that the polarities of the base-drive windings for Q1 and Q2 are opposite, as required to allow only one of the two half-bridge BJTs to be on at a time. C1 (and C4) similarly times the on-time of Q2.

The starting switching frequency is greater than the resonant frequency of the output inductor and lamp. As the lamp conducts, its C6 (C_p) capacitance is 'shorted' by the lamp, leaving the C5 series capacitance (C_s) to resonate with the inductor.

Another similar CFL circuit diagram is shown below. Circuit similarity with the previous unit suggests that CFL circuit design has become optimized for the present technology.

Fluorescent Lamps

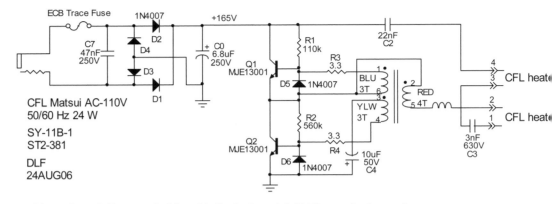

In this unit, a full-wave bridge (4 diodes) and 165 V supply is used.

A third and final CFL inverter circuit is shown below. Note the use of MOSFETs (thereby eliminating the shunt diodes across the BJTs of the previous units), the half-bridge capacitors (0.1 µF, ceramic) in their place, and the additional gate-drive winding.

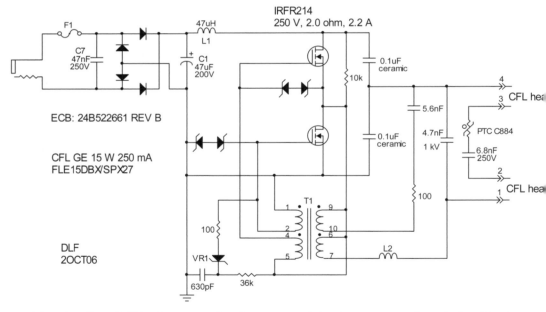

The details of CFL inverter circuits are explained at greater length in Abraham Pressman's book, *Switching Power Supply Design*, (second edition), published by McGraw-Hill in 1998, ISBN 0-07-052236-7, chapter 16. Other chapters in the book also apply directly to CFL inverters. Resonant converters are not simple and to design them well can absorb some learning time.

Repair is otherwise, usually quick. After opening the enclosure, check the fuse (if any) for continuity and then visually inspect the filter capacitors. If they are not bulged at the ends, they are probably okay. Unsolder the transistors and test them, or check them in-circuit with an ohmmeter. (This will not always work because of the base-drive circuit.) Then make sure the inductor has not opened. After this and fuse replacement, there is not much left to fail. Check the diodes, then the base-drive transformer with an ohmmeter for open windings. The base-side electrolytic capacitors can also be suspect. Unless a resistor appears charred, it is probably okay.

Look also for open, fused circuit-board traces. In semi-tropical or tropical environments, look for bugs that have gotten into the lamp and shorted circuitry. After that, you're on your own. The lamp itself, of course, can fail, though usually some indication of a failed vacuum seal or dark regions on the bulb face, if not cracked glass, provides some evidence of that.

CFL lamps are not hard to repair and take little time. They are worth repairing not only for replacement-price savings but also for the familiarity one gains with another household electronics item. You might even adapt a CFL inverter from a unit with a broken lamp to drive a small TFL in a customized household application.

Portable FLs

Portable flashlights or electric torches for emergency use often have FL lighting and are battery-powered. The drivers in these differ from the line-powered drivers in that the typical 6 V battery source requires substantially more voltage gain. One unit I examined had a single-BJT driver-oscillator using a transformer to provide base drive. Instead of heated lamps with filaments, these smaller FLs usually are cold-start and require higher voltages (but no heater power). Consequently, they use transformers with very small turns ratios for a high secondary-winding voltage, are often wound on EE cores, and the bobbins usually have winding separators, to segment the secondary winding so that the voltage across the secondary turns is within breakdown ratings.

Computer LCD-display backlights are a familiar example of portable FLs. The technical literature on them is available on the Internet. Start with the tech-notes written by Jim Williams of Linear Technology Inc. (www.linear.com). Amazingly little technical detail on FLs is available on the Internet from manufacturers; GE appears to be the best. The half-bridge driver is not used in battery-powered FL drivers because of the low voltage. Instead, a push-pull, transformer-coupled oscillator is preferred, called a 'Royer' circuit. The two-transistor oscillator is supplied current from a current source, which can be a small switching converter. Control of drive current thereby controls light output and FL dimming is realized.

One battery-based TFL on the market is shown below. It is sold for emergency lighting because it is not capable of driving the FL directly from the power-line. The power-line only charges the 6 V sealed lead-acid (SLA) battery within it, the source for the FL driver.

Fluorescent Lamps

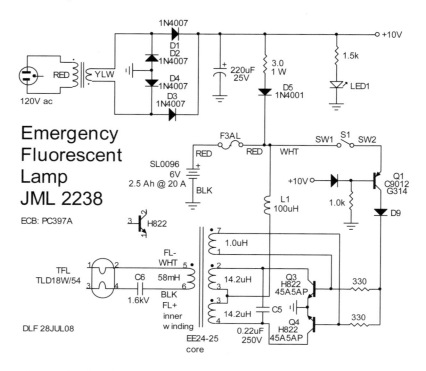

Emergency Fluorescent Lamp JML 2238

ECB: PC397A

DLF 28JUL08

The battery charger is simply a 3 Ω resistor in series with a diode.

Q1 switches base bias to the Royer oscillator BJTs, Q3, Q4, through 330 Ω base resistors. The turns ratio can be calculated from the measurements of the transformer winding inductances. Relative to the primary half-winding,

$$\frac{1}{n} = \sqrt{\frac{L_s}{L_p}} = \sqrt{\frac{58\,\text{mH}}{14.2\,\mu\text{H}}} \approx 64$$

The secondary voltage across the TFL for a 6 V primary voltage is about 383 V peak. When either primary half-winding is conducting, the TFL equivalent circuit is referred to the primary half-winding by n^2 and loads the parallel resonant circuit formed by capacitor C5 with the entire primary winding inductance. The other half-winding couples tightly to the conducting one and leaves only its small leakage inductance in series with C5, thereby involving the inductance of the undriven half-winding. The shunt C5, referred-load combination is across $4 \cdot L_p$, forming a parallel resonant circuit.

The much larger L1, in series with the battery voltage source, provides the oscillator current and because of its relatively large inductance, behaves as though it were a current source for the period of the oscillation. In FL drivers with dimming, this current would be controlled as the dimming variable.

This emergency lamp offers an opportunity for upgrade, to make it operable from the power-line, though not with the existing transformer. A switching supply can easily be placed in the lamp enclosure and the line-operated transformer used to power its control circuits. A three-state charger could even be implemented to extend battery life.

LED Lighting

In contrast to fluorescent lamps, light-emitting diodes (LEDs) are simple to drive and control, yet they have a few subtleties. Some involve how best to use them.

Lights are used generally in two ways: spot and illumination. Spot lighting, as is done with flashlights, under-counter, and track lights, constrains the light to a relatively small solid angle, concentrating it on where it is needed. Illumination is used to light larger volumes such as whole rooms. LEDs in off-grid systems are likely to be used in two distinct applications: fixed-position lighting, such as lights mounted under kitchen counters, and portable lighting: flashlights or electric torches.

The technical literature on FLs and especially LEDs requires some optoelectronics concepts. There are about 680 lumens (lm) per visible watt of light. A 100 W incandescent bulb puts out about 1700 lm. The unit of *luminous intensity* or brightness is the candela (informally a candle of lighting), which is a lumen per steradian, or lm/sr, where the steradian is an area-angle measure, a solid-angle radian. A sphere of radius equal to one (a unit sphere) covers the entire volume of solid angle and has a value of 4π. A steradian covers an area equal to $1/4\pi$ of the surface of a unit sphere. And *illuminance* is luminous flux density with the unit of a *lux* which is a lm/m^2.

Lighting Efficiency

The first electric lighting of any great significance was due to the efforts of Thomas A. Edison's laboratory researchers. Using what now would be regarded as an excessive cut-and-try approach, the right material was found for converting electricity to light. It was small-diameter tungsten wire, heated in a vacuum to avoid oxidation. Tungsten gave off a whitish light and, more significantly, had an operating life of hundreds of hours, extended over time to a thousand or more. At the time of this invention, electronics had not really emerged yet, and none was required for *incandescent* lighting. It was superior to kerosene and natural-gas lighting in maintenance and safety, and quickly replaced it.

Incandescent lamps generate far more heat than light and have poor efficiency as measured in light output per input power, with output units of lumens/watt (lm/W). For the power-limited homesteader, this lighting technology is obsolete. The smaller the bulb, the worse is the efficiency. A flashlight bulb is typically less than 6 lm/W, a 7 W night-light bulb, around 6 lm/W, and a 100 W bulb, 17 lm/W. LEDs are a replacement option for small lights.

Incandescent lighting dominated for the first half of the twentieth century before fluorescent lighting began to supplant it. A 32 W T8 fluorescent tubular lamp outputs 85 to 95 lm/W, five to six times the efficiency of incandescent lamps. Cold-cathode fluorescent lamps (CCFLs) have in recent years become used for laptop computer display backlighting. CCFLs have outputs of typically 40 to 60 lm/W, less than tubular fluorescents but still four to five times the efficiency of incandescents.

High-intensity discharge (HID) lamps such as halogen high-pressure lamps are based on excitation of a light-emitting metallic vapor - much like FLs - and are intermediate in efficiency. A T3 tubular halogen lamp puts out about 20 lm/W.

The latest entrant in the lighting progression is the high-intensity white LED. Despite some impressions, LEDs are not very efficient. At 15 to 20 lm/W, they are only slightly more efficient than large incandescent bulbs. However, for small incandescent applications, such as flashlights, they are three to four times more efficient at the same visible light output. For spot lighting, they also can be the optimal choice, for most LEDs have a limited light distribution angle of around 15 to 25 degrees. Benchtop or desk lighting use can provide higher intensity over the area where needed than a CFL of the same light output. Although CFLs last a long time, LEDs have the longest life of any of the alternative lighting technologies - at least, as projected. (Source: www.otherpower.com)

The Light-Emitting Diode

LEDs have an advantage for those in electronics of being a kind of familiar device. Diode current plotted against voltage is shown below from the component data for a high-intensity white LED, the Vishay TLCW5100, a round, 5 mm diameter device made with indium-gallium-nitride (InGaN) and silicon carbide (SiC) technology. It has a luminous intensity of 4 cd over an 18° angle. This angle is ±9°, marking the off-center angular distance to half-intensity.

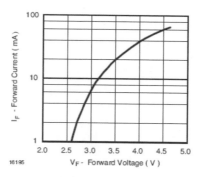

What stands out about LEDs is their higher forward or on voltage than silicon diodes. This LED is rated at 30 mA. From the graph, the corresponding diode voltage is 4.0 V, significantly more than the familiar 0.65 V of low-power silicon diodes. This value is unusually high in that this device uses SiC material.

Another category of LEDs are power LEDs that are often mounted on a heat sink and are rated ≥ 1 W. An example is the 1 W, 6 mm, surface-mount Optek OVSPWBCR4, a white 48 lm emitter with a 120° viewing angle. In contrast to the 5 mm LED above, it is rated to operate at 350 mA with a 1.2 W power dissipation and a voltage of typically 3.6 V, with a 4.0 V maximum.

LED Lighting

The diode curve for LEDs is similar to that of silicon diodes. Above the 'knee' of the exponential curve, current increases much with little change in forward voltage. Therefore, control of current is desired, especially in view of the maximum current ratings which are usually not much higher in power LEDs than the rated operating current. The technology that has emerged for LED drivers is current-output converters for which output current is the controlled variable. Multiple LED driver ICs have come onto the market in recent years. Most are switching converters, often of the boost or switched-capacitor types. All control output current, not voltage.

With current output, multiple LEDs can be placed in series, each conducting the same current. The number of LEDs is limited only by the converter output voltage range.

Flashlight LED Driver

I quickly put together out of available laboratory inventory the following LED driver, based on an 'enduring' converter IC, the RC4193, originally a Raytheon part currently supplied by Fairchild. A search for a newer replacement IC oddly did not produce any meeting the combination of requirements of the application, that of replacing incandescent lamps in flashlights. The 4193 is in an 8-pin DIP package and, alas, did not fit into my intended flashlight housing, though it did light its LEDs. This design can be best applied instead to spot lighting, such as powering over-counter lights.

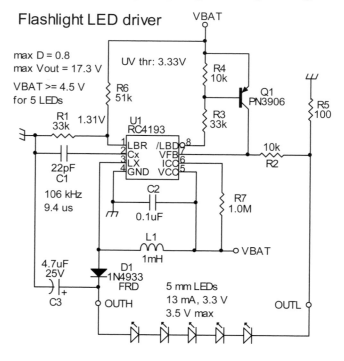

136

This is a *boost* (*common-active* configuration) converter for which the output voltage exceeds VBAT. The LX pin is the single power BJT switch which connects to ground when on, and places VBAT across L1. Inductor current ramps up, t_{on} ends, and the BJT switch turns off, diverting the inductor current through the diode, D1, to the LEDs. R5 is a 100 Ω LED-current sense resistor. The LBR input and /LBD output are low-battery detect pins, used here for undervoltage protection. When VBAT is less than 1.31 V, as set by R1 and R6, then the /LBD output is asserted low, Q1 turns on and pulls the voltage feedback pin (FB) high, turning off the drive. The RC4193 can be upgraded with little modification to an ON Semiconductor (www.onsemi.com) NCP3066. A functionally similar part is the MC34063.

Another direction that can be taken to LED lighting for simple applications avoids the complication of switching supplies. The Infineon BCR402R is a current source for driving LEDs, shown below.

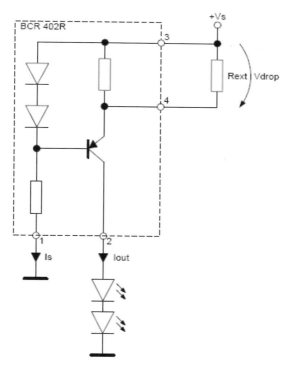

This minimalist solution sets LED current with an external resistor across pins 3, 4. This resistor, in parallel with the internal resistance, has a voltage across it of about one diode drop. As temperature increases, diode voltage decreases at -2 mV/$°$C, thereby tracking LED voltage and reducing LED current and power dissipation. The above circuit can easily be built using discrete components. Its advantage is simplicity; its disadvantage is lower efficiency. For low-power LED drive, it is possibly the best alternative.

Solar Thermoelectric Technology

The search for new energy sources for off-grid electricity includes new methods of conversion of existing sources. There is, in fact, plenty of available energy but it is underutilized due to lack of efficient technology. The sun provides an energy density of about 1 kW/m^2 when overhead on a clear day. How might it be converted to electricity?

Solar Energy: Three Alternatives

Three alternative solutions for the use of solar energy are:

1. **Photosynthesis**: grow crops that can either be burned directly to power a heat engine (such as a steam turbine) and turn a generator or produce biofuel which can be stored, transported, and burned, or used in fuel cells.

2. **Solar Photovoltaic (PV)**: use solar PV panels to convert sunlight to electricity and store it in batteries.

3. **Solar Thermal**: concentrate solar radiation with a collector, heat a fluid, store it in an insulated tank, and drive a thermoelectric converter.

Photosynthesis currently leads the other approaches by a wide margin, as biomass is burned to provide energy in the developing world. Some countries, such as Brazil, are making a significant effort to change from geosourced to ethanol fuel. In the developed world, crops are being grown and converted to biofuels such as ethanol, which can be used to power emerging direct-alcohol fuel cells. For now, solar panels are the dominant attention-getter among alternative-energy enthusiasts. The under $1/W panels, competitive with the power utility grid, were supposed to be here by now. The low-cost technology abandons semiconductor batch processing of solar-cell wafers in favor of extruding a continuous-process ribbon of thin-film amorphous material composed of copper, indium, gallium, and selenium. The ribbon is chopped into panels and used as roofing material. New technology development, as we know, is a nontrivial affair. These panels are now in volume production but the high demand limits availability for home energy. Solar panels still cost an expensive $3.50/W US in 2008, long after promises of cheap PVs.

Solar Thermoelectric System

The problem of electric supply can be decomposed into two problems: energy *generation* and *storage*. With electric output from solar panels, charge must be stored in batteries. This is expensive and cumbersome. It is the *storage* problem that leads to a major advantage of the third alternative, solar thermal. A block diagram of a *solar thermoelectric system* (STES) is shown below.

Solar Thermoelectric System

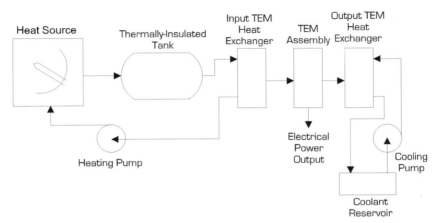

Thermoelectric Conversion

The converter in the above diagram is a *thermoelectric module* (TEM) assembly. More generally, this is some kind of thermoelectric conversion device which converts a temperature differential, ΔT, to electric power, as heat flows from hot side to cold side through it. TEMs are commonly found in car coolers and consist of tens of thermocouples in series. Thermocouples transfer heat by the mechanism of electron diffusion. This is not an efficient process but the efficiency has been increasing as the figure of merit, a quantity denoted by Z, increases. One company, Hi-Z, in San Diego, California (www.hi-z.com), offers TEMs optimized for electricity generation, with a specified efficiency of 4.5 %. This is about 4 % worst-case over the ΔT operating range of the STES. To maintain efficiency, the cold side is held at T_L by a cooling loop using fluid-cooled heat sinks, a small pump, and a cooling pond or radiator and fan. The price of TEMs (from Hi-Z) runs around $7.71/W US, over twice that of $3.50/W US PV panels. For a TE system sizing of 400 W average and peak, the cost of the TEMs is $3084 US.

Solar Thermal Collection

A concentrated solar collector is required to achieve the desired operating temperature (275 °C) of the thermoelectric converter. Three possible collectors are:

- **Dish** - tracks sun in two dimensions with heat collector at the focus of the paraboloid;
- **Trough** - parabolic trough with linear pipe at its focus tracks sun;
- **Heliostat Array** - multiple mirrors track sun in 2D and focus on fixed heat receiver.

Of these three alternatives, the heliostats allow the heat collection to be at the tank, thereby avoiding the need for flexible tubing and a high-temperature pump. However, each of the dozen or so mirrors requires two motors and controls for 2D solar tracking. This solution is not minimal. The dish has temporary appeal because surplus microwave dishes are available, as fiber-optic cable replaces telecom microwave links and large C-band satellite dishes are replaced with smaller ones. The dish surface is covered with low-cost metalized plastic sheeting.

The optimal solution to me appears to be the heliostats, though the trough is a competitor. It too can be constructed with metalized plastic sheeting, and with proper orientation, tracking need only be one-dimensional. The collected thermal energy is stored as a fluid in an insulated tank.

A 400 W average power output requires a thermal input power, or heat rate, of 10 kW for 4 % TEMs. This roughly corresponds to a dish of 12 feet diameter, or 10.5 m² area, a common surplus microwave repeater dish size. (As microwave links are torn down in the US, telecom companies are giving these dishes away for the hauling.) However, the duty-ratio for the sun is about 25 % (when dark skies and seasonal variations are included), increasing collector sizing by 4 times, to 40 kW, or 4 12-foot dishes. A parabolic trough of 10 m² area has dimensions of 1.6 m (5.3 ft) × 6.3 m (21 ft).

A 10 m² concentrating collector using metalized plastic sheeting for reflecting material can be constructed using low-cost building materials for a price of around $1500. By using a parabolic trough with 1D solar tracking, the pipe at the focal line can remain fixed to the storage tank, avoiding the need for high-temperature flexible tubing.

Solar Thermal Storage

Consider the significant cost advantage of thermal versus electrochemical (battery) energy storage. Suppose a fluid with the density and heat capacity of water (4.187 kJ/kg·K) were stored in a 1 m³ tank with R-20 insulation at an average storage temperature of 250 °C. (A spherical tank of 1000 liters, with R-20 thermal insulation, results in a 6 °C/day loss of temperature, which is 300 W of continuous loss.) The tank has a diameter of 1.24 m (4.0 ft), about the size of a household appliance. The stored energy, useable over 100 °C, is

$$Q = \left(4.187 \frac{kJ}{kg \cdot K}\right) \cdot \left(1 \frac{kg}{l}\right) \cdot (1\,kl) \cdot (100\,K) = 419\,MJ = 116\,kW \cdot h$$

This assumes a worst-case ambient temperature of 50 °C. An insulated tank of this size would cost around $200 US with mounting and plumbed ports.

At 250 °C, the working fluid in the heating and storage loop cannot be liquid water. A sodium-potassium alloy is a possibility. So are some high-temperature synthetic oils. Additionally, fluid properties for heat transport can be optimized by using a different storage material in the tank optimized to store heat. The available energy of a substance due to its differential temperature above ambient is the *sensible* heat, because it can be 'sensed' by measuring its temperature. A substance that undergoes a state change also changes internal energy to change molecular reconfiguration. This *latent* heat can be substantial. (This is why snow on roads is plowed instead of melted.) A material that is optimized for storing latent heat is a *state-change material* (STM). Suppose that the cost of the fluid and the optionally additional STM is about 50 % of the tank cost. Then the total heat storage system cost is about $300 US. Because the tank volume is not large, a slightly larger tank using a lower-performance fluid or STM is an attractive cost tradeoff.

Solar Thermal and PV Costs Compared

The TE approach succeeds based on the assumption that solar energy collection and storage is relatively cheap, thereby supporting inefficient TEM generation. Output power is dc and requires an inverter, but those are low-cost commodity items. (Even the better sine-wave inverters are affordable, though not cheap yet.) And they are not a major factor in STES feasibility. Solar PV also requires an inverter.

The output-referred energy storage for the above 400 W system is 5.22 kW·h. At 400 W average output, it will last 13 hours, or about a half a day. Add $320 for the cooling loop, and the total cost of the 400 W, 5 kW·h STES is about $5,200.

For comparable energy storage in a battery bank, the output energies must be compared. The size of the battery bank, using 12 V, 50 A·h (600 W·h) deep-cycle batteries at $75 US each, has 9 batteries and costs $675 US, or about twice as much for storage. When battery-bank replacement is considered - perhaps every 10 years - the 20-year cost is over 4 times. In addition, the batteries require somewhat more maintenance than a thermal storage system.

The lower cost of solar thermal collectors over PV panels is negated by the high cost of TEMs. For a 400 W PV system, the input power need only be 400 W/(0.25), or 1600 W, assuming no battery charger loss. The PV panel cost, with tracker (to get 0.25 solar availability), is about $6,400, resulting in a total PV comparison cost of $7,100, or $1,900 (27 %) more than the STES. When the system is scaled up to 1 kW output, the advantage of the STES grows to 37 %.

TE Feasibility

The STES mechanical (moving) components are heliostat motors, a small pump, and possibly a cooling fan. The PV system has only the panel tracking. The two are roughly comparable in amount of maintenance. Why, then, with the lower cost of the STES, has it not become the preferred supply solution? The answer is that high-Z TEMs are only now becoming commercially available. Perhaps another reason is that alternative-energy distributors are familiar with PVs and do not yet know about STESs because they are not yet commercially available for distribution. This leaves the home-energy builder an option that is not yet commercially available: your own solar thermoelectric system.

TE Conversion Devices

Solar thermoelectric system (STES) feasibility has been examined and found to be favorable in cost compared to solar PV. The critical component of the system is the thermoelectric conversion device which was assumed to be the existing, still emerging, technology of thermoelectric modules, based on thermocouples.

Thermoelectric Modules

TE modules are commercially available, though TEMs optimized for electric generation are new and undergoing significant improvement. An assembly of 72 14 W TEMs in series provide 1 kW electric output power. Each assembly provides 8 A at 118.8 V, operating at maximum power conversion, with an efficiency of 4.5 %. This low efficiency relative to PV modules (which are typically around 15 %) is more than compensated by the low cost and simplicity of thermal energy storage. A relatively large amount of thermal energy can be stored in a relatively small tank. (See 'Solar Thermal Storage'.) A fluid with the heat capacity (4187 J/kg·K) and density (1 kg/l) of water stores sensible heat of 4.187 kJ/l for each °C above ambient temperature, or 4.187 MJ/m^3. For a $\Delta T = 250$ °C, the available heat stored per cubic meter is 1.047 GJ.

A TEM suitable for STES design is the Hi-Z HZ-14. A Thevenin equivalent circuit model of it is a 3.5 V source in series with a 0.15 Ω resistance, as shown below.

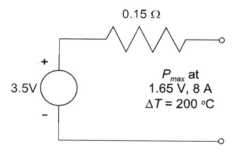

This equivalent circuit was derived from the HZ-14 characteristics shown below.

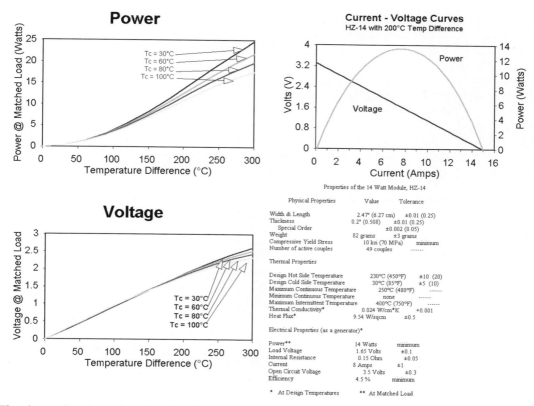

The thermal voltage is related to the ΔT across the TEM by the *Seebeck coefficient*, α, in volts per kelvin, V/K;

$$v_\theta = \alpha \cdot \Delta T$$

The TEM output voltage is

$$v_o = v_\theta - i \cdot R = \alpha \cdot \Delta T - i \cdot R$$

Electric output power,

$$p_o = v_o \cdot i = \alpha \cdot \Delta T \cdot i - i^2 \cdot R$$

The thermal input power,

Solar Thermoelectric Technology

$$p_i = \dot{Q}_i = G_\theta \cdot \Delta T$$

where G_θ is the TE thermal conductance;

$$G_\theta = \frac{k_\theta \cdot A}{l}$$

and k_θ = TE thermal conductivity, A = TEM heat-flux cross-sectional area, and l = TEM thickness. Then the power conversion efficiency is

$$\eta = \frac{p_o}{p_i} = \frac{\alpha}{G_\theta} \cdot i \cdot \left(1 - \frac{i}{I_0}\right)$$

Where

$$I_0 = \frac{v_\theta}{R} = \alpha \cdot \frac{\Delta T}{R}$$

η is maximum at $v_\theta/2$, as shown in the graph below.

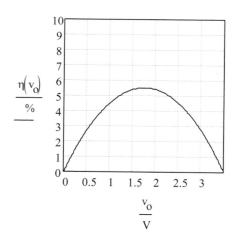

Output power is also maximum at $I_0/2$ and $v_\theta/2$.

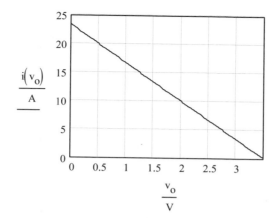

The efficiency coefficient becomes a figure of merit, Z;

$$Z \cdot \Delta T = \frac{\alpha}{G_\theta} \cdot I_0 = \left(\frac{\alpha^2}{G_\theta \cdot R} \right) \cdot \Delta T$$

The geometric expressions for both thermal and electrical conductance have the same form;

$$G = \frac{k \cdot A}{l}$$

A and l are the cross-sectional TEM area and thickness for both thermal and electrical G. For electrical $G\ (= 1/R)$, $k = \sigma$, and for thermal G, $k = k_\theta$. Substituting and solving for Z,

$$Z = \frac{\alpha^2 \cdot \sigma}{k_\theta}$$

The quest to increase Z is to that of finding more efficient TE materials. The search is well beyond elemental metals because their electrical and thermal conductivities track. At present, manufactured TEMs are dominated by semiconductor materials such as bismuth telluride. What is needed to significantly increase Z is a material with a large α - highly electrically conductive but thermally insulative.

The plot of i versus v_o with ΔT as the parameter is shown below, where

$$i = \frac{v_\theta}{R} \cdot \left(1 - \frac{v_o}{v_\theta}\right)$$

As ΔT increases, the maximum power and current increase linearly by increasing v_θ.

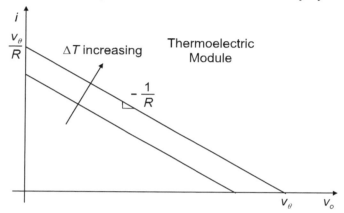

The operating ΔT for the HZ-14 TEMs is chosen to be from 150 °C to 250 °C. Consequently, the available thermal energy from the tank is over this temperature range of 100 °C. The useable stored energy is consequently 418.6 kJ/l·K $\equiv$ 418.6 MJ/m^3·K. For a 500 gallon (1.893 m^3) tank, the useable stored energy is 792 MJ, or 220 kW·h.

Under full input ΔT and unloaded, the assembly of 72 HZ-14 TEMs connected electrically in series has an open-circuit voltage of 252 V. Inverters or converters must be rated for this open-circuit voltage. The full 72-TEM stack also has a total internal resistance at P_{max} of 10.8 Ω.

Thermionic and Thermotunneling Devices

Another kind of thermal-to-electric conversion transfers heat by *thermionic* emission. The heat and charge transfer mechanism is not electron diffusion as it is for thermocouples but is ballistic. Electrons take a ballistic path through an electric field, as in thermionic valves (or vacuum tubes, as Americans call them), in which the emitting surface must be heated. The energy required for electrons to leave a surface is related to the work function of the material. Metals have too high of a work function for ambient thermionic conversion, but semiconductors are feasible. Electrons flow from the hot to the cold electrode. An external load reduces voltage across electrodes to less than the open-circuit voltage that opposes electron flow, and power is converted. One research group expects a doubling of efficiency over thermocouples. While for thermoelectric devices, figure of merit, Z, is at best around 1, for thermionic devices it is in the range of 2 to 5. Ballistic transport carries more heat than diffusion.

There is yet another promising device in the works. *Thermotunneling* devices are based on a third heat and charge transfer mechanism, the quantum effect of tunneling, as occurs in tunnel diodes. Conceptually, this kind of device seems almost too good to be true; separate two flat metal plates 10 nm apart, and coat the emitting plate with a low work-function material, to enhance tunneling. At that spacing, electrons tunnel from one plate to the other, carrying heat with them. The problem in practice is the close spacing. (Thermionic transport occurs at an optimal spacing of ten times as much, around 100 nm.) Semiconductor processes are used to create two surfaces with matching nonuniformities over the tunneling surface. The close spacing relative to the dimensions of plate area results in localized shorts which decrease efficiency. Prototypes are claimed by www.powerchips.gi to have shown 15 % efficiency, three to four times that of TEMs. (Also, see the parent company at www.borealis.com.)

A problem shared by thermionic and thermotunneling devices is that the narrow barrier causes thermal conductivity to be high, resulting in large heat flow for a given current. The problem is being addressed for semiconductor thermionics by the University of Tennessee-Oak Ridge National Labs effort, by using multiple barriers in series that cause thermal resistance to add.

Closure

Thermal-electric conversion should be interesting in coming years, as revolutionary new devices become commercially available. At the projected efficiencies, not only might solar thermal electric generation be competitive with existing power generation technologies, vapor-compression refrigeration and the internal combustion engine might also be heading for replacement. The current state of development for thermionic and thermotunneling devices has gone sufficiently far to establish their basic feasibility. What remains is plenty of engineering refinement and then novel applications for these new devices.

Other major power-conversion technologies under development are thermophotovoltaics (TPV), which greatly increases PV efficiency by making use of infrared energy through frequency conversion to silicon PV frequencies using an optical processing layer, and the re-emergence of efficient and low-ΔT Stirling engines.

INDEX

148

Royer inverter, 131, 132

S

Samlex, 21
Schottky diode, 65, 73
Schumacher, 64, 65
SCR, 41, 65, 66, 67
Seebeck coefficient, 143
semi-discrete design, 28
sense resistor, 7, 9, 37, 46, 51, 73, 80, 137
SG3525A, 28, 42, 43, 44
shoot-through, 48, 70
skin effect, 54
small-ripple approximation, 38
snubber, 34, 35, 36, 37, 73, 100, 117
solar charger, 5, 6
solar thermoelectric system (STES), 138
speed voltage, 87
stall torque, 89
state-change material (STM), 141
Stirling engines, 147
switching frequency, 15, 19, 73, 76, 83, 114, 118, 129

T

thermionics, 147
thermistor, 51, 57
thermoelectric module (TEM), 139
thermophotovoltaics, 147
thermotunneling, 147
three-state charging, 63, 64, 67
TL071, 9, 10, 11
TL431, 65, 66
TL494, 28, 51, 56, 57, 70, 76

torches, electric, 131, 134
torque, 22, 26, 86, 87, 88, 89, 90, 91, 92, 93, 94, 95, 96, 97
torque constant, 87
Trace Engineering, 6
transductor, 80, 81
transfer switch, 3
triangle-wave, 117
trickle charge, 63
turns ratio, 15, 34, 35, 45, 53, 54, 55, 68, 72, 75, 78, 83, 93, 114, 131, 132

U

undervoltage protection (UVP), 41
utilization, 30, 118

V

VEC034, 49, 51
VEC050D, 21, 53, 54, 56, 60
VEC1095, 67, 70, 73, 80
Vector Mfg., 6, 21, 53, 54, 67
voltage constant, 25, 52, 87, 96
voltage doubler, 9, 129

W

Williams, Jim, 131
wind converter, 92, 96, 97, 98, 119
wind generator, 86, 96, 97
wind speed, 94
winding dots, 30

X

Xantrex C-60, 5, 6, 12